wagamama

ways with noodles

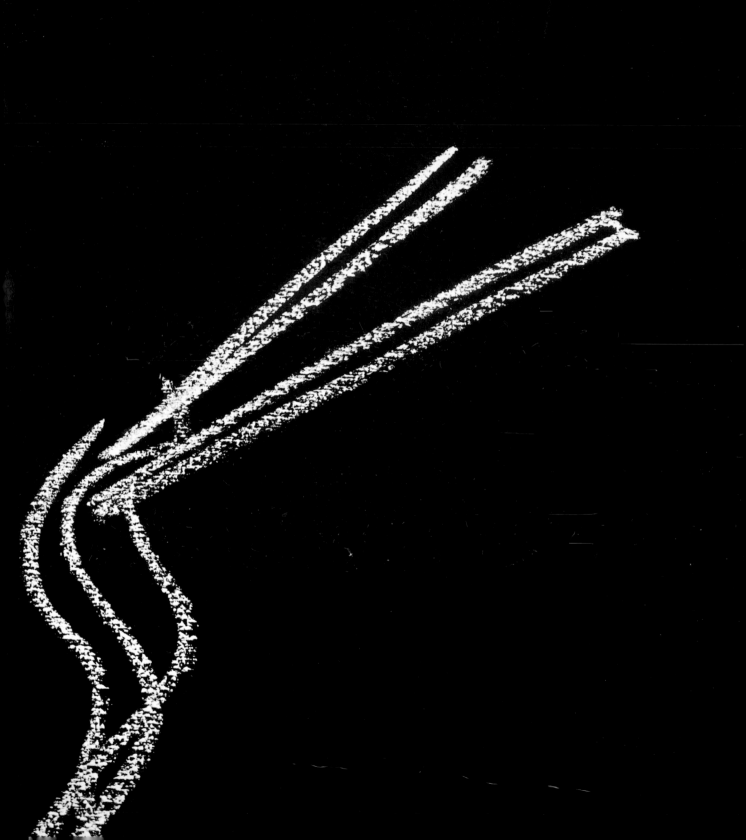

wagamama

ways with noodles

Hugo Arnold

METRO BOOKS
NEW YORK

METRO BOOKS
New York

An Imprint of Sterling Publishing
387 Park Avenue South
New York, NY 10016

ISBN 978-1-4351-5188-8

For information about custom editions, special sales, and premium and corporate purchases, please contact Sterling Special Sales at 800-805-5489 or specialsales@sterlingpublishing.com.

Manufactured in China

2 4 6 8 10 9 7 5 3 1

www.sterlingpublishing.com

Author Hugo Arnold   **Project editor** Jennifer Wheatley   **Photographer** Ditte Isager   **Art direction and design** Lucy Gowans
Food stylist Jacque Malouf   **Props stylist** Tabitha Hawkins   **Copy editor** Stephanie Evans   **Editorial assistant** Vicki Murrell
Production David Hearn and Nic Jones

contents

noodles, topping, broth…

this is where we started.
it defines what wagamama is all about.
a bench. a bowl. nutritious food.
speedy service. satisfaction. simplicity.

We are wild about noodles. Sure, we do rice dishes—and adore them too—but noodles are what really get us going. wagamama may be known for *ramen*, but our enthusiasm doesn't stop there; stir-fries, salads, quick ones, child-friendly ones. There really is no end to the variations.

Noodles epitomize fast food. They are easy to prepare and utterly versatile. It might be *ramen* or soup tonight, stir-fry tomorrow, and the next night something more like a stew. We like to call these one-pots. The topping might be meat or fish or vegetables—sometimes a combination of all three.

Cooking noodles is simple. They are invariably softened in boiling unsalted water, refreshed under cold water, then combined with other ingredients. Which also makes them fast. And easy to control. If you like more chile, less ginger, or lots of garlic, it is easy to dress your noodles accordingly. Or not at all. Some people like to dip their noodles in sauce, and why not?

You may like a thick noodle, or a thin one. It is up to you to choose. We have some rules, but they are not very strict. You may not be able to make a *gyoza* out of a strip of *udon* noodle, but there is nothing wrong with substituting *ramen* for *somen*, if that is what you prefer.

Noodles have been eaten for centuries, and while the debate continues over whether noodles or pasta came first, we like to keep

East. It is something about the soy and ginger, the fresh mint and greens that we find hard to resist. One bowl containing these ingredients is enough to refresh and invigorate, soothe and comfort.

Whereas Italy seeks variety through shape, Asia provides interest through type: egg, rice, wheat, buckwheat, beanthread, and potato. Uses vary, but as with any cuisine there are preferred partners and techniques (see pages 8–9). Noodles provide infinite combinations of taste, texture, and flavor, given the various starches they contain. They partner with ease, never complaining, always willing. Try beef with black beans and egg noodles, then the next time with rice noodles. You may have a preference (we certainly do), but both work equally well. As do egg or buckwheat noodles in spiced duck, asparagus, and noodle soup (along with a healthy dose of soy, cilantro, and toasted sesame seeds).

Noodles are central to Asian cuisine. They stretch through Japan, Korea, China, Vietnam, Thailand, Malaysia, and into Indonesia, turning up in soups, side dishes, as nests or packaging for meat, fish, or vegetables, as beds for curry, or in a salad. They can be stir-fried or dressed, or poached in a heady broth, with aromatics provided by freshly chopped herbs.

Add convenience to this versatility. Most noodles have a shelf-life of at least a few weeks—longer if they are dried. They are inexpensive, easy to cook, and nutritious. No wonder they are found in such diverse settings as remote mountain villages in China, downtown Tokyo, and the beaches of Thailand.

Noodles are the fast food of today. You can stir-fry in minutes, conjure a broth in less time than it takes to make a cup of tea, even fashion a salad in mere moments. And they are nothing if not healthy: high in complex carbohydrates, low in fat, and essentially free from additives, while most if not all recipes make much use of fresh vegetables. The emphasis on fish and only a small quantity of meat is in keeping with dietary advice of the twenty-first century.

At wagamama noodles are a way of life: fun—sexy, even. Slurping noodles is one of those simple pleasures. The sort that leaves you with a smile of satisfaction. In our restaurants we encourage the slurping, a practice that is considered proper in Japan. Whether you want to slurp at home is entirely up to you, but these recipes provide ample opportunity whichever way you decide to go.

noodle knowledge

Noodles excel in a soup and get dressed in a sauce with real style. They come hot. They come cold. They are dipped in sauces, deep-fried, wrapped, and, on occasion, are fashioned into nests for other ingredients. They come fat and thin, and are made from rice, wheat, and even beans and potatoes. They are quick, versatile, and healthy—a perfect food in many ways. They also calm and restore. And excite.

At wagamama we use the word *ramen*, which refers to the noodle, but also to the bowl where the noodle is combined with broth and vegetables and often fish or meat. Sometimes it may include all of these ingredients—as in wagamama *ramen*, a dish that we are rather proud of. *Ramen* is pretty key at wagamama. Served at noodle stalls throughout Asia, this hot, fresh, tasty, near-instant food is what started the wagamama way.

Noodles are very like pasta. Their shape is not crucial, but it does help. How you cook them is important too. In a *ramen* you want the starch in the noodle to combine with the broth. In a dish where the noodle is dressed, you want the starch inside the noodle to stay there. That way the dressing sticks and everyone is happy. Including the noodle.

Noodles have soul; they need to be handled carefully. Not timidly, but with respect. Noodles don't like salted water for example. The seasoning should happen in the dish. It's just their way. Some like to be boiled, others are happy in hot water. Almost all like to be precooked, which makes your job so much easier. And quicker.

You can be neat and tidy with noodles, but it's much more fun not to be. At wagamama we like to slurp—it feels more relaxed. What's more, the oxygen enhances their flavor. We are often asked how we decide on which noodle to use. The answer is not easy. We could say it doesn't matter too much. But it does. Sort of.

Rice ones (1) Often called rice-stick noodles, but also vermicelli. The difference is thin or really thin. The latter only require soaking in hot water to soften and are then used in salads, soups, and stir-fries. Rice-stick noodles, or "sticks," as they are known, come as medium and wide. If this sounds a bit confusing, it is, not helped by each noodle company seemingly at odds over what is medium and wide. There are also the really wide ones, which are used in stir-fries. Rice noodles tend to suit lighter dishes such as those with a broth rather than a heavy sauce. Gluten-free and wheat-free, they are usually sold dried, in nests.

Wrapping ones (2) Some call them wontons, we call them *gyozas*. But they all amount to the same thing: wrappers. You might call them sandwiches, but that would be missing the point. These are generally rather more delicate—a thin skin covering anything from meat to fish to vegetables and even noodles (see the slippery ones below). You can bake, steam, deep-fry, or boil these noodles according to your mood, or to what stuffing you are using. Wrappers or skins come in wheat and rice versions and are also known as spring roll wrappers or skins. Buy fresh or frozen.

Bucking ones (3) Buckwheat lends a brown-gray color to noodles, and a wonderful nutty flavor. In Korea they call them *naengmyon;* in Japan they are known as *soba*. These noodles are often served cold, and are dipped in sauces for breakfast in Japan. But they also turn up in soups. There are some who think *soba* noodles work in salads, but they need careful handling. They need lots of other ingredients and a good dressing or they can show up too worthy, too healthy by far. We are all for healthy eating. But it should be fun too. Buckwheat noodles are usually sold dried and the 100 percent buckwheat version have the virtue of being gluten-free and wheat-free.

Slippery ones (4) Often referred to as cellophane noodles, but also as beanthreads, these crunchy, slippery, translucent, gelatinous strands deliver little in the way of flavor but bags of texture. The trick is to get the typically light sauce to coat each strand, that way they perform as noodles (lumps are not a good thing when it comes to noodles). Also fantastic in salads, cellophane noodles are sold dried.

Wheaty ones (5) The richness of egg noodles is not always what you are looking for, particularly when the other ingredients are high in the protein stakes. Wheat noodles are said to be the oldest form of Chinese noodle, and have a firm but somewhat silky bite. In their thin form (*somen*) they find their way into soups. The thicker version (*udon*) gets dressed in rich dishes where the heart and soul is as much in the sauce as the other ingredients. *Udon* noodles are fat, white, unctuous, slippery, and utterly delicious. They turn up in soups of a robust nature and a few stir-fries. Wheat noodles are sold dried (the *somen* often delightfully wrapped).

Eggy ones (6) These come both thick and thin, and are the typical, some might say archetypal Chinese noodles. They have a rich firm texture, not unlike egg pasta come to think of it. But we would not suggest that you substitute one for the other. Pasta for noodles that is. The process is different—which will be explained later. *Ramen* are classed as eggy noodles and have a defined place in Japanese cooking (see facing page). Available both fresh and dried.

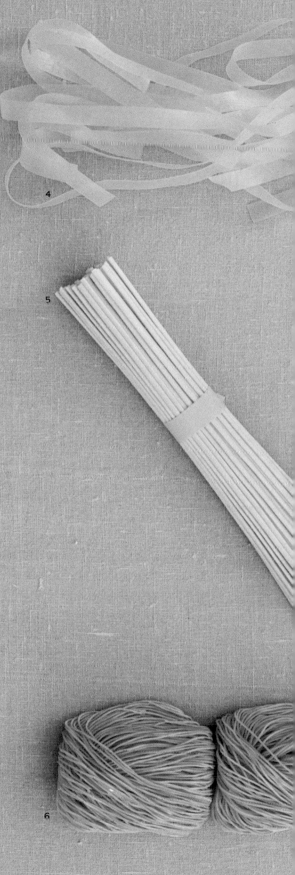

ingredients

Chinese flowering chives
Stronger than normal chives and flat rather than round-stemmed. Often referred to as garlic chives. Available in Asian markets. If substituting normal chives, double up on the quantity.

Dashi
A light fish stock made from *konbu* (see right) and dried bonito flakes.

Dashi no moto
An instant powdered version of *dashi*, commonly used in domestic kitchens in Japan.

Enoki mushrooms
Tight clusters of long-stemmed, creamy-colored mushrooms, enoki should retain a crunchy texture when cooked correctly. The flavor is delicate rather than full-bodied.

Fermented black beans
Salted black soybeans, traditionally used as a seasoning. You can buy them preprepared.

Fish sauce (nam pla)
A thin liquid extracted from salted, fermented fish. It deteriorates once opened and darkens with age. Fish sauce should be light golden brown with a tangy and salty flavor.

Flowering greens (choy sum)
A type of brassica related to bok choy and mustard greens. The flower looks pretty in cooked dishes.

Galangal
Galangal is from the same family as ginger but has a drier taste and is significantly more peppery and spicy. You can substitute one for the other, but be aware of their differences.

Hoisin sauce
Thick, dark, and spicy, this soy-based sauce is easily obtainable.

Kaffir lime leaves
The leaf of a citrus tree. Dried or frozen ones are practically useless. Buy fresh and store in the fridge, wrapped in plastic wrap.

Kamaboko-aka
Japanese fishcakes, bought in rolls (see photograph on page 176), which are traditionally white with a pink outer crust. Available from Asian markets.

Katsuo bushi
Dried fish flakes from the bonito fish (similar to tuna). You can add to salads or directly onto finished dishes, but it is most commonly used to make *dashi* (see left).

Kimchee
Korean in origin, *kimchee* is pickled vegetables, most often Chinese cabbage, and fish. Most Koreans make their own, but you can buy commercial versions in Asian markets.

Konbu
Sold both dried and ready soaked, *konbu* is kelp seaweed. It delivers a fruity saltiness to dishes.

Mirin
Sake that is combined with sugar, so it has a sweet, tangy flavor. It's used in small quantities to give a smooth roundness to dishes.

Miso
Miso varies enormously from one brand to another. Essentially a paste made from fermented soybeans and combined with other ingredients. General all-purpose *miso*, made with brown rice, has a big, rich flavor while sweet white *miso* is much lighter and more delicate. It is best to experiment until you find one you like.

Oyster sauce
Thick, dark, and brown, this meaty-flavored sauce is made from a concentrate of oysters cooked with soy sauce. It is used both in cooking and as a condiment. For vegetarians there is an alternative made with mushrooms. Widely available.

Rice vinegar
Usually a light bronze color, rice vinegar typically tastes sweet and mildly sour rather than sharp.

Sake
See page 187.

Shichimi or seven-spice pepper
A hot kick of chile and black pepper combined with sesame, hemp, and poppy seeds as well as orange zest and *nori* seaweed. Widely available in Asian markets, this seasoning gives an extra kick, particularly to *soba* and *udon* dishes.

Shiitake mushrooms
Available in both a fresh and dried form. When fresh, the flavor is quite muted with a pleasant crunchy texture. When dried, the flavor is much more concentrated and meaty and the texture is more firm. If dried, they generally need to be soaked in hot water for 15 to 20 minutes.

Soy sauce
Light soy sauce is generally best for cooking and is suitable for most of the recipes in this book. Dark soy sauce gives a stronger color and flavor and can also be used as a condiment.

Thai basil
Purple-stemmed but with green leaves. Thai basil has a strong anise flavor, which both sweetens dishes and adds a welcome aroma. Available from Asian markets.

Tofu or bean curd
Made from soybeans, tofu is rich in protein. There are essentially two kinds, firm and silken. The former is the one to use if any cooking is involved, the latter if it is being dressed and used in a salad or similar style of dish.

Yellow bean sauce
A mixture of yellow beans and salt, thickened with flour. It comes in two versions, whole beans and crushed or broken beans. The latter tends to be saltier. Available in Asian markets.

stocks and preparations

It is impossible to overemphasize the importance of good stock. It is a yardstick against which chefs are measured. In Japan, for example, a miso soup is a defining dish. A stock has to work on many levels, to satisfy so many criteria. It has to be well seasoned, but not too much. It has to be sweet, but not cloying. It has to have body, but only when it is in balance with everything else.

All this requires time, a commodity most of us severely lack. At wagamama we get around the issue by making stock in large batches to our own specification. This is not really possible at home, though, hence the recipes that follow.

Taking shortcuts is not something we entertain. But then we are not looking to try to put food on the table in the same way as you are. We may deliver dishes in minutes, but hours of work beforehand go into making that possible. What is important about the quicker versions of these stocks is that you realize what you are going to get. Something less, certainly, but also an experience that is tailored to the circumstances at the time.

There is nothing wrong with bouillon cubes. But not all cubes are the same. Some taste decidely better than others. And there are other useful stock products out there. Fresh stock sold in cartons for example, or powder granules. What makes one good, or better, than another? Only you can decide.

As you work your way through this book you will find the recipes involve preparation that is then followed by the cooking. At first this may seem an odd way of working, frustrating even, as little seems to be happening. In practice, however, this route is tried and tested.

other bits and pieces

How you chop is very important. Avoid right angles; they are difficult on the eye. And in the mouth. Diagonal slices are pleasing to look at and expose a greater surface area to heat and to other flavoring ingredients. Generally a good thing.

A wok is useful. But not essential. A skillet will also work. There is no need to rush out and buy the kit. A fork, after all, will do the job of chopsticks. Only differently.

Stir-frying is different from frying. You cook over a high heat. And quickly. Moving everything around. Either by tossing or using a scoop. Don't fall shy of this technique. It is key.

These dishes have generally been specified for two people on the basis that a meal will be made up of two or three dishes. You might, of course, choose to double up one recipe for four. There are no hard-and-fast rules. It depends rather on what you like.

chicken stock (1) *when you're not in a hurry*
2¼ pounds chicken bones • ¾ pound pork bones • 1 onion, peeled and chopped • 2 carrots (scant ½ cup), chopped • 4 leeks (¾ pound), sliced • 2½ tablespoons sliced fresh ginger • 4 Chinese cabbage leaves, roughly chopped

Put the meat bones in a large pot, cover with cold water, and bring almost to a boil. Turn the heat right down and simmer for 2 hours, skimming off any froth that rises to the surface.

Add the vegetables and another 1 quart of water and bring almost to a boil again, then lower the heat and simmer for another hour. Remove from the heat and let cool. Strain off the liquid, return to the pan, and simmer for 1 hour to reduce further. Season with the chicken stock seasoning below.

chicken stock seasoning
2 teaspoons salt • 2 teaspoons sugar • small pinch of white pepper 1 teaspoon *dashi no moto* (see page 11)

chicken stock (2) *when you need to make stock at the same time as cooking*
2 good-quality chicken bouillon cubes • 1 pound uncooked chicken thighs or wings • 1 leek, finely chopped • 1 carrot, finely chopped • 1 quart water

Combine all the solid ingredients in a pan, add the water, and bring almost to boiling point. Lower the heat and simmer for 30 minutes. Strain and proceed.

chicken stock (3) *when you want something to eat now!*
2 good-quality chicken bouillon cubes • 1 leek, finely chopped • 1 carrot, roughly chopped • 1-inch piece of fresh ginger, roughly chopped • 1 quart water

Combine all the solid ingredients in a pan, cover with the water, and bring to a boil. Strain and proceed.

vegetable stock (1) *when you're not in a hurry*
1 pound potatoes • 1 small sweet potato • 2 carrots • ½ small butternut squash, seeded • 1 white onion • 1 red onion • 4 Chinese cabbage leaves • 1 leek • 2 tablespoons canned tomatoes • 3 quarts water

Peel the root vegetables, squash, and onions, then roughly chop all the vegetables. Put in a large pot with the water. Bring to a boil, then lower the heat to a gentle simmer and cook, uncovered, for 3 hours. Turn off the heat, let cool, and strain. Season with the vegetable seasoning below.

vegetable stock seasoning
2 teaspoons salt • 2 teaspoons sugar • pinch of white pepper

vegetable stock (2) *when you need to make stock at the same time as cooking*
2 good-quality vegetable bouillon cubes • 2 Chinese cabbage leaves 2 carrots, roughly chopped • few sprigs of flat-leaf parsley • 3 quarts water

Place all the ingredients in a large pot and bring to a boil, then lower the heat and simmer for 10 to 15 minutes if you have time, then strain.

wagamama

sauces

You can dip, dress, marinate, soak, or season with a sauce. You can use a lot or a bit, it's all up to you. Which we rather like. A sauce can come out of a container, and some of the best do. But making your own is not only enjoyable, it also gives you control. Soy sauce may be one to buy. Barbecue sauce on the other hand tends to be rather better when fashioned in your own kitchen.

The same is true of a green or red curry paste. Fresh ingredients pounded together tend to sing in a way that those in a container do not. It is something about the care, love, and attention. There is likely to be more of that in your kitchen than a factory. At least, that's what we've found.

All these sauces are good keepers. Fridge-friendly, they will happily sit things out for a while and then add zest and spice to a dish on demand. Maybe a dish that calls for them directly, or another one that does not. You never quite know how useful a good sauce can be. A dipping sauce, for example, does not always need to be dipped into. A splash or two over a bowl of *ramen* noodles can make for interesting eating.

You'll find other sauces in this book linked to specific dishes. In general these are more tailored to individual recipes, but this doesn't mean they can't be used elsewhere. After all, if you like a sauce, it seems a shame not to eat it.

sweet chili dipping sauce

makes about ¾ cup

½ pound red chiles, trimmed
3 garlic cloves, peeled and roughly
    chopped
½ cup light brown sugar
2 teaspoons white wine vinegar
scant 1 teaspoon salt

In a small saucepan, combine everything in a small pan with ⅓ cup water, bring to a boil, and simmer over medium heat until soft, about 5 minutes. Blitz in a blender and season with the salt. Return to the pan and simmer for another 10 minutes, taking care not to let it catch on the bottom. Let cool, cover, and refrigerate.

Many store-bought sweet chili sauces deliver too much sweetness and not a lot of character in the chile, two things that you maintain control over when you make this all-purpose sauce at home. It will last indefinitely in the fridge and is, according to some, rather good on a bacon sandwich in place of ketchup.

red curry paste

makes enough for 2 to 3 recipes

10 dried red chiles, soaked in
    hot water and roughly chopped
1 ¼-inch piece of fresh ginger or
    galangal, peeled and finely
    chopped
2 lemongrass stalks, outer leaves
    removed, finely chopped
finely grated zest of 2 limes
1 tablespoon finely chopped
    cilantro stems
1 tablespoon chopped shallots
1 tablespoon chopped garlic
1 teaspoon light brown sugar
salt and white pepper
vegetable oil

Pound each ingredient, adding them one after the other, in a pestle and mortar. Season with salt and pepper and stir in enough oil to form a paste.

You can always buy curry pastes (red and green), but none will be as fresh-tasting and invigorating as making your own. This will last for a few weeks in the fridge covered with a slick of vegetable oil.

yasai soba dressing

makes about 1 cup

¾ cup teriyaki sauce, home-made
    (see page 19) or bought
⅓ cup yellow bean sauce
1 lemongrass stalk, outer leaves
    removed, finely sliced
1 tablespoon peeled and grated
    fresh ginger

In a small bowl, combine all the ingredients until well blended.

You can dress noodles with this sauce, or put a blob on the side or top of a dish. You can dip a gyoza in it, or add a bit to a salad dressing. It's very Asian in taste and attitude. It will keep for months in the fridge.

green curry paste

makes about ⅔ cup

6 green chiles, roughly chopped

1 lemongrass stalk, outer leaves removed, thinly sliced

3 kaffir lime leaves, finely sliced

½-inch piece of fresh ginger, peeled and grated

bunch of cilantro, stems finely chopped (leaves reserved for another dish)

1 teaspoon cumin seed, roasted in a hot, dry skillet

2 garlic cloves, peeled and roughly chopped

1 tablespoon finely chopped shallot

1 teaspoon shrimp paste (available from Asian markets)

1 tablespoon vegetable oil

Blitz all the ingredients in a blender or food-processor or pound in a pestle and mortar to a fine paste.

As with the red version (see page 16), making this at home ensures a vibrant lively paste that will make no end of difference to your finished dish. You can buy green curry paste, but it rarely makes the grade. At least we don't think so. This will keep indefinitely in the fridge.

chili ramen sauce

makes about ½ cup

2 scant teaspoons sugar

2 tablespoons malt vinegar

3 tablespoons store-bought sweet chili sauce

5 tablespoons fish sauce (*nam pla*)

In a small pan, dissolve the sugar in the vinegar over gentle heat. Let cool, and then combine with the other ingredients.

Using sugar as a seasoning is widely practiced in Asia and this sauce is no exception. It brings a real meatiness to dishes and is generally lightly drizzled over food. It will keep for several weeks in the fridge.

teriyaki sauce

makes about ½ cup

½ cup sugar
4 tablespoons light soy sauce
2 tablespoons sake
1 teaspoon dark soy sauce

In a small saucepan, heat the sugar and light soy sauce over low heat and stir until the sugar has dissolved. Simmer until thick, 5 minutes, add the sake and dark soy sauce, and let cool.

This sauce is most commonly used to brush meat with so that it can marinate before it is broiled. You can also use it as a dipping sauce or to drizzle over noodles in broth. It will keep for a few weeks in the fridge.

barbecue sauce

makes about ¾ cup

⅓ cup store-bought yellow bean
    sauce
⅓ cup store-bought hoisin sauce
2 teaspoons sugar
2 garlic cloves, peeled and minced
1 tablespoon toasted sesame oil
pinch of white pepper
1 tablespoon dark soy sauce
2 tablespoons light soy sauce

Combine all the ingredients in a small bowl.

There are lots of brands of barbecue sauce, each one with its advocates. Making your own allows for variation (alter the amounts of each ingredient used) but most importantly makes you realize how bright and vibrant this sauce can be. Keeps in the fridge for several days.

kare lomen sauce

makes about ½ cup

2 lemongrass stalks, outer leaves
    removed, roughly chopped
1-inch piece of fresh galangal,
    peeled and roughly chopped
2 garlic cloves, peeled and finely
    chopped
2 onions, peeled and roughly chopped
1 red bell pepper, seeded and
    roughly chopped
1 teaspoon sweet paprika
1 teaspoon fennel seeds
½ teaspoon chili powder
½ teaspoon turmeric
½ teaspoon curry powder
1 teaspoon shrimp paste
    (available from Asian markets)

Combine all the ingredients in a blender or food-processor and blitz to a smooth consistency.

This is a bright and invigorating sauce (see picture on left). It has a Thai theme with all that lemongrass and galangal. It will keep for a few days in the fridge.

tori kara age sauce

makes about 3 cups

1-inch piece of fresh ginger, peeled
    and grated
3 cups light soy sauce
3½ tablespoons sake
1 teaspoon sugar
1 tablespoon oyster sauce

In a saucepan, combine all the ingredients and heat gently to dissolve the sugar. Set aside to let cool.

Ginger and soy, soy and ginger. The combination is a winning one whichever way you say it. This is a marinade, a dipping sauce, and something to drizzle over pretty much anything, from grilled or broiled fish and meat, to noodles sitting in a scant broth with or without other things. Keeps for several weeks in the fridge.

chili sauce

makes about 1¼ cups

2 tablespoons vegetable oil
2 lemongrass stalks, outer leaves removed, finely chopped
1 teaspoon peeled and grated fresh ginger
1 chile, finely chopped
1 red onion, peeled and finely chopped
2 garlic cloves, peeled and finely chopped
½ teaspoon salt
½ teaspoon sugar
1 tablespoon light soy sauce
1 red bell pepper, seeded and finely chopped
1 tablespoon store-bought sweet chili sauce
1 tablespoon ketchup
1¼ cups water

In a small saucepan, heat the vegetable oil over low heat until hot. Add the next 8 ingredients and sauté for 7 to 8 minutes without coloring. Add the red bell pepper and continue cooking gently for 8 to 10 minutes. Add the remaining ingredients, bring to a boil and simmer for 10 minutes. Blitz in a blender or food processor and use.

There is a rounded fruitiness to this sauce allied to a hefty kick, which, if you choose, you can down-play simply by reducing the amount of chile used. Generally used as a dipping sauce. It will keep for a few days in the fridge.

soy dipping sauce

makes 2 servings

2 tablespoons soy sauce
1 tablespoon water
½ teaspoon sugar
½ teaspoon peeled and grated fresh ginger
2 shallots, finely chopped
dash of toasted sesame oil

In a small bowl, combine all the ingredients, stir to dissolve the sugar, and serve.

Light, bright, and full of interest, this sauce is for dipping certainly, but can also be used as a finishing sauce for other dishes. Keeps for several weeks in the fridge.

sweet miso dressing

makes about ½ cup

2 tablespoons *mirin* (see page 11)
2 tablespoons sake
4 tablespoons sugar
110g *miso* paste (see page 11)
1 tablespoon chili oil
1 tablespoon vegetable oil
2 teaspoons *shichimi* (see page 11)

In a small saucepan, combine the *mirin* and sake and bring to a boil. Lower the heat, add the sugar, and stir until dissolved. Pour onto the *miso* paste in a small bowl and beat until smooth. Add the oils and *shichimi* and mix thoroughly.

Miso brings a deliciously meaty quality to dishes. Here it is used in a dressing, so it is designed to enhance dishes. But a dish of noodles dressed in this sauce makes for quite a nice snack. It will keep for several days in the fridge.

gyoza sauce

makes about 1½ cups

1 large garlic clove, peeled and
    finely chopped
1 large red chile, finely chopped
salt
2 tablespoons sugar
½ cup malt vinegar
1 cup light soy sauce
1 tablespoon toasted sesame oil

Mash the garlic and chile together with a little salt with the side of your knife to form a paste. In a small saucepan, dissolve the sugar in the vinegar over low heat. Combine everything and store in a sealed container.

A great dipping sauce. It also adds interest to finished dishes and is good for dipping grilled or broiled fish and meat into. It will keep for several weeks in the fridge.

souped up

wagamama *ramen* is the sort of food wagamama was built on. Noodles and a delicious broth along with some select vegetables and meat. Easy to cook. Simple to serve. Delicious. And good for you.

We cannot claim to have invented this combination. It has existed in the East for centuries. Noodle stalls are an original fast food source. Maybe the original fast food. Simplicity at its best.

It is easy to soup things up. We do it all the time. But only once in a while do we come up with a real winner. A few of these appear in the following pages. What makes a soup win? It's something to do with satisfaction. A licking of the lips. A sigh of contentment.

Noodles have this effect. Particularly when the broth is good. You can cut corners with the broth. Some do. But we don't advise it. This is the one chapter when a really good stock will show off its best. This is not to forget the other ingredients. But don't skimp on the stock.

What is your soup about? If you don't know, how are your noodles expected to? There needs to be a plan. Which is why we are very careful when working on new soups. A wagamama *ramen* is quite hard to beat, or at least to equal. Which is sort of where our benchmark lies. A marker that makes us happy. Proud even.

A word about your bowls. We use *ramen* bowls, which are large, wide, and made from melamine. This allows you to pick them up, the closer to slurp from without burning your hands. Any big bowl will suffice. It rather depends on how much slurping you wish to do.

tofu and miso soup with somen noodles

serves 2

3½ ounces *somen* noodles
2 tablespoons vegetable oil
salt and white pepper
3½ ounces firm tofu, cut into
    ½-inch cubes
1 red onion, peeled and finely
    sliced
1 small potato, peeled and
    thinly sliced
1 medium carrot, grated
1 red chile, seeded and finely
    sliced
1 green chile, seeded and
    finely sliced
1 cup chicken stock (see
    page 13)
2 tablespoons white *miso* paste
    (see page 11)
1 tablespoon soy sauce
1 sheet of *nori* seaweed
2 scallions, white part only,
    thinly sliced (to serve)

Soften the noodles according to the instructions on the package, drain, and refresh under cold water.

In a hot wok, heat 1 tablespoon of the vegetable oil. Season the tofu and stir-fry until golden on all sides, remove, and drain on paper towels.

Heat the remaining oil in the wok, add the red onion and potato, and stir-fry over medium heat for 2 minutes. Add the carrot and red and green chiles, and cook for another minute. Add 1 cup water, the chicken stock, *miso* paste, and reserved tofu. Season with soy sauce and salt and pepper.

Bring to a boil, reduce the heat, and simmer until the potato is cooked, about 5 minutes.

Meanwhile, cut the *nori* into strips. In a dry skillet, cook over medium heat to crisp up, a scant minute.

Divide the noodles into 2 bowls, pour over the soup, and serve topped with the slices of *nori* and scallions.

tofu, lettuce, and egg noodle soup

serves 2

3½ ounces egg noodles
4 tablespoons vegetable oil
salt and white pepper
3½ ounces tofu (smoked if
    possible), cut into ½-inch cubes
1 carrot, peeled and julienned
2 scallions, finely sliced
1 tablespoon finely sliced shallot
2 garlic cloves, peeled and
    finely sliced
2 cups vegetable stock (see
    page 13)
1 teaspoon soy sauce
2 teaspoons fish sauce (nam pla)
scant teaspoon sugar
2 teaspoons mirin (see page 11)
1 small head of Bibb lettuce,
    shredded

Cook the noodles according to the instructions on the package, drain, and refresh under cold water. Heat the wok on high heat and add 2 tablespoons of the oil. Season the tofu and fry until golden brown on all sides. Remove and drain on paper towels.

Wipe out the wok and return to the heat. Add the remaining oil, then stir-fry the carrot, scallions, shallot, and garlic until the carrot is tender, about 2 minutes. Add the vegetable stock, soy sauce, fish sauce, sugar, and *mirin* and bring to a boil. Add the lettuce and season with salt and pepper to taste.

Divide the noodles and tofu between 2 bowls, ladle over the hot soup, and serve.

three-mushroom soup

serves 2

2 dried shiitake mushrooms
3 ounces ramen noodles
2 teaspoons vegetable oil
1 carrot, peeled and finely sliced
2 teaspoons finely sliced shallots
2 ounces enoki mushrooms,
    broken up
⅓ cup sliced button mushrooms
handful of baby spinach
handful of snow peas, thinly sliced
1¼ cups chicken stock (see
    page 13)
1 sheet of konbu (kelp) seaweed
2 teaspoons soy sauce
½ teaspoon sugar
2 teaspoons rice vinegar
1 teaspoon miso paste (see
    page 11)
scant 2 teaspoons sesame seed,
    briefly toasted in a hot,
    dry skillet

In a small, heatproof bowl, pour ⅔ cup boiling water over the mushrooms and let soak.

Cook the noodles according to the instructions on the package, drain, and refresh under cold water.

In a hot wok, heat the oil and stir-fry the carrot and shallots for 5 minutes. Drain the shiitake (reserving the liquid), and discard any tough stems. Slice thinly and add them to the wok with the other mushrooms, spinach, and snow peas. Continue to stir-fry for another 3 minutes.

Bring the stock to a boil, adding the liquid from the mushrooms. Add the *konbu*, soy sauce, sugar, rice vinegar, *miso*, and noodles to the wok and toss well so that everything is combined. Pour in the boiling stock and bring to a boil.

Divide between 2 bowls, and serve scattered with the toasted sesame seed.

spring greens and seafood soup with pickled ginger

serves 4

7 ounces flat egg noodles
1 tablespoon vegetable oil
1 carrot, peeled and julienned
2 lemongrass stalks, outer leaves
      removed, finely chopped
1 chile, finely sliced
2 garlic cloves, peeled and sliced
2 kaffir lime leaves
7 ounces skate fillet
1 cup chicken stock (see page 13)
2 tablespoons rice vinegar
3½ ounces peeled raw shrimp,
      deveined
4 sea scallops, shelled, trimmed,
      and sliced horizontally in half
2 handfuls of spinach
1 small head of Bibb lettuce, shredded
salt and white pepper
pickled ginger

Cook the noodles according to the instructions on the package, drain, and refresh under cold water.

In a hot wok, heat the oil and stir-fry the carrot, lemongrass, chile, garlic, and kaffir lime leaves for 1 minute. Add the skate, chicken stock, and rice vinegar and reduce the heat. Poach the skate, turning halfway through, until it just comes away from the bone, 5 minutes. Remove and let cool. As soon as you can handle it, slide the meat off the bones.

Add the shrimp, scallops, spinach, and lettuce to the hot stock. Season with salt and pepper. Cook over low heat until the scallops and shrimp are cooked through and the leaves wilted, 3 to 4 minutes. Add the noodles and skate to the pan and toss so that everything is well combined and heated through.

Ladle into 4 bowls and serve topped with pickled ginger.

seafood and egg noodle soup

serves 4

1 tablespoon vegetable oil
1 red onion, peeled and thinly sliced
2 garlic cloves, peeled and minced
2 lemongrass stalks, outer leaves
      removed, finely sliced
1⅓ cups thinly sliced button
      mushrooms
½ teaspoon sugar
2 teaspoons fish sauce (nam pla)
1 quart chicken stock (see page 13)
8 sea scallops, shelled and trimmed
8 raw, unpeeled shrimp
16 mussels, scrubbed and
      debearded
finely grated zest and juice of 1 lime
3½ ounces medium egg noodles
1 red chile, sliced
2 teaspoons toasted sesame oil
3 scallions, thinly sliced

In a hot wok, heat the vegetable oil, and stir-fry the onion, garlic, lemongrass, and mushrooms for 1 minute. Add the sugar, fish sauce, and chicken stock and bring to a boil.

Add the seafood and return to a boil. Add the lime zest and juice, the noodles, and the chile. Simmer until the noodles are tender, the seafood is cooked, and all the mussels are open, about 3 minutes. Discard any mussels that remain closed.

Divide among 4 bowls, drizzle over the sesame oil, and scatter over the scallions.

hot and sour seafood broth

serves 2

5 ounces raw shrimp, peeled
  and deveined, shells reserved

1 quart vegetable stock (see
  page 13)

1 green chile, seeded and finely
  sliced

salt and white pepper

6 kaffir lime leaves

2 lemongrass stalks, smashed

3½ ounces rice noodles

1 small cleaned squid, cut into rings

1 tablespoon fish sauce (nam pla)

juice of 1 lime

6 shiitake mushrooms, stems
  removed, thinly sliced

2 scallions, thinly sliced

6 cooked crab claws, cracked

2 tablespoons roughly chopped
  cilantro

In a saucepan, combine the shrimp shells, stock, chile, ½ teaspoon salt, lime leaves, and lemongrass and bring to a boil. Reduce the heat, cover, and simmer for 30 minutes. Strain into a clean pan.

Cook the noodles according to the instructions on the package, drain, and refresh under cold water.

Mix together the shrimp, squid, fish sauce, lime juice, mushrooms, and scallions. Season with salt and toss gently.

Bring the strained broth back to a boil. Add the shrimp and squid mixture along with the crab claws and simmer for 2 minutes. Taste and correct the seasoning if required.

Place the soaked noodles in 2 bowls and ladle over the hot broth. Serve scattered with the cilantro leaves.

prawn and quail egg soup

serves 2

6 raw, unpeeled shrimp

2 cups chicken stock (see
  page 13)

2 teaspoons mirin (see page 11)

1 tablespoon soy sauce

2 teaspoons sake

1¼-inch piece of fresh ginger,
  peeled and julienned

1 garlic clove, peeled and finely
  sliced

3½ ounces rice vermicelli

handful of snow peas

2 heads of bok choy, separated
  into leaves

4 quail eggs

salt and white pepper

2 scallions, finely sliced

large handful of cilantro leaves

Remove the shells (and heads if available) from the shrimp, devein, and set the shrimp aside. In a saucepan, combine the shells (and heads) with the stock, mirin, soy sauce, sake, ginger, and garlic and bring to a boil. Simmer for 10 minutes, then remove the shrimp shells.

Soak the vermicelli according to the instructions on the package, drain, and refresh under cold water.

Cook the snow peas and bok choy in the stock until cooked, about 5 minutes. Add the shrimp, simmer for a scant 2 minutes, and remove from the heat.

Divide the vermicelli between 2 bowls and add the shrimp and vegetables. Poach the quail eggs in the remaining broth over medium heat for 2 minutes and spoon them over the other ingredients, along with the stock. Check the seasoning and serve scattered with the scallions and cilantro.

hot and sour seafood ramen

serves 2

for the marinade

2 teaspoons fish sauce (*nam pla*)
2 teaspoons *mirin* (see page 11)
2 teaspoons soy sauce
dash of Tabasco
2 teaspoons cornstarch

¾ pound raw, in the shell, unpeeled,
    mixed seafood, such as shrimp,
    sea scallops (trimmed),
    small clams (well rinsed
    and drained), or mussels
    (scrubbed and debearded)
salt and white pepper
3 ounces *ramen* noodles
1½ cups chicken stock (see
    page 13)
1 cinnamon stick
3 cloves
1 tablespoon rice vinegar
1 teaspoon sugar
1 red chile (or to taste), finely
    sliced
2 teaspoons fish sauce (*nam pla*)
½ cup baby corn, halved lengthwise
½ cup zucchini, thinly sliced
6 pieces of pickled bamboo
    shoots (*menma*)
1 tablespoon *wakame* seaweed,
    soaked in warm water for
    5 minutes, drained, and
    roughly sliced
4 scallions, finely sliced
few sprigs of watercress

Make the marinade: In a medium bowl, whisk the fish sauce, *mirin,* soy sauce, and Tabasco into the cornstarch. Season the seafood with salt and pepper and add to the marinade, coating well. Cover and set aside for an hour; overnight in the fridge is even better.

Cook the noodles according to the instructions on the package, drain, and refresh under cold water.

In a large saucepan, bring the chicken stock, cinnamon, cloves, rice vinegar, sugar, chile, and fish sauce to a boil and add the seafood, marinade, baby corn, and zucchini. Simmer until the seafood is cooked and all the shells are open, about 3 minutes. Discard any shells that remain closed.

Divide the noodles between 2 bowls, top with the seafood and vegetables, and ladle in the stock. Check the seasoning and serve topped with the bamboo shoots, *wakame*, scallions, and watercress.

3½ ounces *ramen* noodles

1 medium egg

½ cup all-purpose flour

vegetable oil, for frying

2 garlic cloves, peeled and chopped

1 leek, sliced

½ cup snow peas

1 carrot, peeled and thinly
    sliced on the diagonal

1 onion, peeled and sliced

2 teaspoons soy sauce

1 tablespoon rice vinegar

1 tablespoon fish sauce (*nam plu*)

2 star anise

2 cups chicken stock (see page 13)

10 raw, peeled shrimp, deveined

2 teaspoons toasted sesame oil

store-bought sweet chili sauce

crispy shrimp ramen soup

Cook the noodles according to the instructions on the package, drain, and refresh under cold water.

In a medium bowl, lightly whisk the egg with ⅓ cup iced water. Sift in the flour and barely combine to make a smooth batter (don't overwork it, or it will become heavy).

In a hot wok, heat 1 tablespoon of oil and stir-fry the garlic, leek, snow peas, carrot, onion, soy sauce, rice vinegar, fish sauce, and star anise for 2 minutes. Pour in the chicken stock, bring to a boil, and simmer for 5 minutes.

In a wok or deep-sided pan, heat 1¼ inches of vegetable oil to 350°F. Drop in a bit of batter to test the temperature; if it bubbles up and turns golden, you are ready to go. Dip each shrimp in the batter (you won't require all of it) and fry until crisp and golden, 30 seconds to 1 minute. Remove and drain on paper towels.

Ladle the soup and noodles into 2 bowls, ensuring there is an island of noodles surrounded by broth. Drizzle with the sesame oil and top with the shrimp. Serve with the chili sauce.

serves 2

5 ounces firm tofu

vegetable oil, for frying

½ pound *ramen* noodles

4 slices of *kamaboko-aka* (see
    page 11)

4 crabsticks

1 egg, hard-boiled

4 cooked, peeled shrimp

2 heads of bok choy, roughly
    chopped

1 quart chicken stock (see page 13)

2 boneless, skinless chicken breasts

salt and white pepper

12 pieces of pickled bamboo
    shoots (*menma*), drained

1 tablespoon *wakame* seaweed,
    soaked in warm water for 5
    minutes, drained, and chopped

2 scallions, sliced

wagamama ramen

Cut the tofu into ½-inch slices. In a skillet, heat a bit of vegetable oil and fry the tofu until just colored on each side, about 1 minute.

Cook the noodles according to the instructions on the package, drain, and refresh under cold running water. Divide between 2 bowls along with the *kamaboko-aka*, crabsticks, tofu, half an egg each, 2 shrimp each, and the bok choy.

In a saucepan, bring the chicken stock to a boil. Preheat the grill or broiler or a grillpan. Lightly coat the chicken breasts in vegetable oil, season with salt and pepper, and grill, broil or chargrill until cooked, about 4 minutes each side. Let rest for 5 minutes and slice on the diagonal into ½-inch strips.

To serve, pour the chicken stock over the noodles, lay the chicken strips on top, and garnish with the *menma, wakame,* and scallions.

If we have a signature dish, then this is it; pure wagamama. Broth, noodles, and a host of toppings, so lots of variety. This is the only recipe you'll also find in The wagamama Cookbook. *We are rather proud of it.*

crab and wonton broth

1 medium, cooked crab
vegetable oil
salt and white pepper
1 carrot, peeled and roughly
    chopped
1 celery stalk, roughly chopped
1 onion, peeled and roughly
    chopped
2 cups chicken stock (see
    page 13)
3½ ounces rice vermicelli
2 large eggs, 1 separated,
    1 lightly beaten
½-inch piece of fresh ginger,
    peeled and minced
2 teaspoons finely chopped
    scallion
1 garlic clove, peeled and minced
small bunch of cilantro, leaves
    picked, stems finely chopped
8 wonton wrappers/skins
2 small heads of bok choy, leaves
    trimmed and separated
handful of snow peas
3½ ounces carrots, peeled and cut
    into ¼-inch dice
3½ ounces celery root, peeled
    and cut into ¼-inch dice
2 teaspoons soy sauce

Preheat the oven to 400°F. Crack the crab shell with the back of a large knife. Pick the crabmeat, keeping the white and brown meat separate. Discard the "dead man's fingers."

Place the crab shells in a roasting pan, toss with a bit of vegetable oil, season well with salt, and roast for 20 minutes. Transfer to a saucepan, add the carrot, celery, and onion and pour over the chicken stock. Bring to a boil slowly, skim, and simmer for 30 minutes, skimming the surface as necessary. Stir in the egg white, simmer for 5 minutes, then turn off the heat.

Line a strainer with a double layer of cheesecloth, pour the stock through, and let drain into a clean saucepan. (This may sound like quite a performance, but it means you will have a clear stock in the finished dish, which looks and tastes very impressive.)

Combine the brown crabmeat with the egg yolk, ginger, scallion, garlic, and the chopped cilantro stems. Season with salt and pepper to taste.

Place a teaspoon of this crab mixture in the center of 4 of the wonton wrappers. Dab the edges with the beaten egg, cover with a second skin, and seal, pushing out as much air as you can. Poach the wontons in boiling salted water for 5 minutes, drain, refresh under cold water, and set aside. Blanch the bok choy and snow peas in the same water for about 15 seconds, drain, and refresh under cold water.

Cook the vermicelli according to the instructions on the package, drain, and refresh under cold water.

Now blanch the carrots and celery root in boiling salted water for 1 minute, refresh under cold water, and transfer to 2 bowls. Add the wontons and vermicelli and cover with the clear broth. Add the bok choy and snow peas and sprinkle with the white crabmeat. Season with the soy sauce and serve.

marinated salmon ramen

serves 2

for the marinade

1 ¼-inch piece of fresh ginger,
    peeled and grated
2 teaspoons *mirin* (see page 11)
2 teaspoons soy sauce
2 teaspoons fish sauce (*nam pla*)

2 salmon fillets, about 5 ounces
    each
salt and white pepper
3½ ounces *ramen* noodles
2 cups chicken stock (see
    page 13)
2 teaspoons fish sauce (*nam pla*)
2 garlic cloves, peeled and minced
1 carrot, peeled and julienned
½ cucumber, seeded
    and julienned
2 ounces green beans, trimmed
    and halved lengthwise
handful of cilantro leaves

In a medium bowl, combine the marinade ingredients. Season the salmon fillets with salt and pepper and add to the marinade. Turn to coat several times, cover, and set aside for 1 hour; overnight in the fridge is even better.

Cook the noodles according to the instructions on the package, drain, and refresh under cold water.

In a large saucepan, combine the chicken stock with the fish sauce and garlic and bring to a boil. Add the salmon and its marinade, cover, and simmer for 2 to 3 minutes. Add the carrot, cucumber, and beans and simmer until the fish is just cooked, about another 2 to 3 minutes. Remove the fish and keep warm.

Divide the noodles between 2 bowls. Pour over the soup, ensuring each bowl gets an equal share of vegetables. Check the seasoning. Top with the fish and serve scattered with cilantro leaves.

vietnamese-style crab noodle soup

serves 2

7 ounces rice vermicelli
1 tablespoon fish sauce (*nam pla*)
1 teaspoon sugar
salt and white pepper
1 quart chicken stock (see
    page 13)
5 ounces lump crabmeat, flaked
1 small head of Bibb lettuce, finely
    shredded
2 teaspoons finely sliced scallion
½ cup bean sprouts
1 lime, cut into wedges

Cook the vermicelli according to the instructions on the package, drain, and refresh under cold water.

In a saucepan, combine the fish sauce, sugar, and a generous pinch of salt with the stock. Bring to a boil, lower the heat, and simmer gently for 20 minutes.

Add the crabmeat, check and adjust the seasoning if necessary, and remove from the heat.

Divide the noodles between 2 bowls. Ladle the soup over the noodles, top with the lettuce, scallions, and bean sprouts and serve with the lime wedges.

marinated sea bass with green vegetables and ramen noodles

serves 4

for the marinade
2 teaspoons soy sauce
1 tablespoon toasted sesame oil
2 teaspoons fish sauce (*nam pla*)
2 teaspoons *mirin* (see page 11)
2 teaspoons cornstarch

7 ounces sea bass (branzini) fillets
       (skin on), cut into 1¼-inch
       pieces
salt and white pepper
3½ ounces *ramen* noodles
1 quart chicken stock (see
       page 13)
2 garlic cloves, peeled and minced
1¼-inch piece of fresh ginger,
       peeled and grated
1 tablespoon fish sauce (*nam pla*)
1 tablespoon rice vinegar
juice of 1 lime
handful of green beans, trimmed
2 tablespoons frozen peas,
       defrosted
handful of spinach
handful of cilantro leaves

Make the marinade: Combine the soy sauce, sesame oil, fish sauce, and *mirin*. Stir in the cornstarch to dissolve. Combine the fish with the marinade ingredients and season with salt and pepper. Cover and set aside for an hour; overnight in the fridge is even better.

Cook the noodles according to the instructions on the package, drain, and refresh under cold water.

In a saucepan, combine the chicken stock, garlic, ginger, fish sauce, rice vinegar, and lime juice and bring to a boil. Blanch the beans in this mixture until just tender, about 4 to 5 minutes. Remove with a strainer or tongs and refresh under cold water.

Add the fish pieces and marinade to the simmering stock, bring to a boil for 2 minutes, then add the beans, the peas, and spinach to the pan with the noodles and simmer for another minute. Check the seasoning.

Divide among 4 bowls and serve scattered with cilantro leaves.

chargrilled chicken, soba, and miso soup

serves 2

for the marinade

2 teaspoons hoisin sauce

1 teaspoon fish sauce (*nam pla*)

1 teaspoon *mirin* (see page 11)

1 boneless, skinless chicken breast

3 cups chicken stock (see page 13)

1 tablespoon red *miso* paste (see page 11)

1¼-inch piece of fresh ginger, peeled and thinly sliced

2 garlic cloves, peeled and sliced

7 ounces *soba* noodles

2 heads of bok choy, roughly chopped

1 large hard-boiled egg, shelled and halved

Make the marinade: In a medium bowl, combine the hoisin sauce, fish sauce, and *mirin*. Add the chicken breast and toss well. Cover and set aside for an hour; overnight in the fridge is even better.

Preheat the grill or grillpan. Chargrill or charbroil the chicken until cooked, about 4 or 5 minutes each side.

In a saucepan, combine the chicken stock, *miso* paste, ginger, and garlic and bring to a boil. Add the *soba* noodles and bok choy and cook until the noodles are just tender, about 3 minutes.

Divide the soup between 2 bowls, ensuring each has an equal share of noodles. Slice the chicken on the diagonal and place on the noodles and broth. Top with half a hard-boiled egg and serve.

hot and sour chicken ramen

serves 2

for the marinade

2 teaspoons *mirin* (see page 11)

1 tablespoon fish sauce (*nam pla*)

1 red chile, thinly sliced

1 garlic clove, peeled and minced

5 ounces dark chicken meat (leg and thigh), trimmed and roughly chopped

salt and black pepper

3 cups chicken stock (see page 13)

2 star anise

1 cinnamon stick

1 tablespoon rice vinegar

1 teaspoon honey

2 heads of bok choy, sliced

3 ounces *ramen* noodles

few sprigs of cilantro

Make the marinade: Mix the ingredients in a medium bowl. Add the chicken, season with salt and black pepper, and toss so that everything is well combined. Cover and set aside for 1 hour; overnight in the fridge is even better.

In a saucepan, heat the chicken stock along with the star anise, cinnamon, rice vinegar, and honey. When boiling, add the chicken and its marinade, bok choy, and the noodles. Bring back to a boil and simmer until the chicken is cooked, about 3–4 minutes. Remove any froth from the surface of the water.

Divide between 2 bowls and serve topped with the cilantro.

chili pork ramen

serves 2

2 lean pork steaks
2 tablespoons barbecue sauce
    (see page 19)
3½ ounces thin *soba* noodles
2 cups chicken stock (see
    page 13)
1 tablespoon chili *ramen* sauce
    (see page 18)
bunch of cilantro, leaves picked
large handful of bean sprouts
1 small red onion, peeled
    and thinly sliced
1 red chile, seeded and
    thinly sliced
1 lime, cut into wedges
teriyaki sauce (see page 19)

Combine the pork with the barbecue sauce in a plastic food bag, massage, and set aside for 1 hour; overnight in the fridge is even better.

Preheat the grill or broiler. Grill the pork until cooked, about 3–4 minutes each side. Let rest and then slice on the diagonal.

Cook the noodles according to the instructions on the package, drain, and refresh under cold water.

In a saucepan, heat the chicken stock. Combine the noodles, chili *ramen* sauce, cilantro leaves, bean sprouts, onion, and chile and divide between 2 bowls. Ladle over the hot stock, top with the sliced pork, and serve with a lime wedge and the teriyaki dipping sauce.

This recipe is by Sjoerd Hoek, from wagamama in Amsterdam.

pork, shrimp, and egg noodle soup

serves 2

3½ ounces medium egg noodles
2 tablespoons vegetable oil
2 garlic cloves, peeled and
    thinly sliced
2 ounces ground pork
2 ounces raw, peeled shrimp,
    deveined
3 cups chicken stock (see
    page 13)
1 tablespoon fish sauce (*nam pla*)
2 Chinese cabbage, stems removed
    and leaves cut into rough strips
salt and white pepper (optional)
2 teaspoons toasted sesame oil
2 scallions, thinly sliced
½ cup bean sprouts
1 tablespoon cilantro leaves
1 tablespoon roasted peanuts
1 lime, cut into wedges

Cook the noodles according to the instructions on the package, drain, and refresh under cold water.

Heat a small skillet over medium heat, add 1 tablespoon of the vegetable oil, and fry the garlic until crisp and golden, about 1 minute. Toss the garlic and the hot oil through the noodles and reserve.

Heat a heavy-bottom pan over medium heat, add the remaining oil, and cook the ground pork until it begins to brown, about 5 minutes. Add the shrimp, the stock, and fish sauce and bring to a boil. Add the cabbage and simmer for 30 seconds, check and correct the seasoning if necessary, and remove from the heat.

Divide the garlic noodles between 2 bowls, ladle over the soup, and add the sesame oil. Top with the scallions, bean sprouts and cilantro leaves. Sprinkle with the chopped peanuts and serve with the lime wedges.

clear beef noodle soup with tashima

serves 2

2 sheets of *tashima* (dried kelp) seaweed

3½ ounces *udon* noodles

3½ ounces beef (boneless top loin steak)

2 cups chicken stock (see page 13)

salt and white pepper

1 teaspoon soy sauce

1 scallion, sliced

1 garlic clove, peeled and crushed

Cut several thin strips of the seaweed and reserve. Soak the rest in warm water for 30 minutes. Drain, rinse carefully, and cut into 2-inch lengths.

Cook the noodles according to the instructions on the package, drain, and refresh under cold water.

Cut the beef into bite-size pieces. In a saucepan, bring the stock to a boil. Season the beef with salt and pepper and add to the stock, stirring to ensure the meat isn't stuck together. Add the soy sauce, scallion, and garlic and skim off any impurities. Reduce the heat and simmer for 10 minutes. Add the noodles and simmer for another 5 minutes. Add the soaked seaweed and check the seasoning.

Divide between 2 bowls, top with the reserved seaweed strips, and serve immediately.

rich beef noodle soup

serves 2

for the stock

1¼ pounds beef bones

14 ounces pork bones

2 star anise

1 cinnamon stick

1¼-inch piece of fresh ginger, peeled and sliced

1 onion, peeled and quartered

3½ ounces *udon* noodles

2 tablespoons vegetable oil

2 garlic cloves, peeled and finely sliced

1 tablespoon finely sliced shallots

7 ounces boneless sirloin beef steak, trimmed and very thinly sliced

2 tablespoons soy sauce

2 tablespoons fish sauce (*nam pla*)

salt and white pepper

handful of bean sprouts

large handful of cilantro leaves

large handful of mint leaves

Combine all the stock ingredients in a pan, cover with 2½ quarts cold water, and bring to a boil. Periodically skim off the froth that will form on the surface to stop the broth going cloudy. Simmer for 2 hours. Strain into a clean saucepan, bring back to a boil, and reduce by half, about 30 minutes. You should have about 2¾ cups of the rich stock.

Cook the noodles according to the instructions on the package, drain, and refresh under cold water.

In a hot wok, heat the oil and sauté the garlic until golden; remove and set aside. Add the shallots and stir-fry until golden and crisp, remove, and add to the garlic.

Divide the noodles between 2 bowls. Add the beef, soy sauce, and fish sauce to the broth and simmer until the beef is just cooked, about 2 minutes. Check the seasoning.

Ladle the beef and stock over the noodles. Serve topped with the bean sprouts, cilantro, mint, and crispy garlic and shallots.

Simmering the stock for 2 hours may sound like a stage you might want to skip, but it is the essence of this dish.

W

wrapped

You normally dress a noodle. Or soak it in a broth. But there is a way that turns this notion on its head. Wrapping noodles do that. Round or square, they envelop a neat pile of deliciousness. This might be vegetables. Usually there is protein too. Typically minced, or cut small. With some you dip. With others all the punch is contained within. In others still, the noodle not only wraps but turns up in the filling too. Usually these are the slippery ones (see page 9).

Wrapped noodles make great finger food. Packaging you can and do want to eat. They work on picnics, shine at parties, and generally encourage a pretty relaxed view about eating. If you steam or boil, you end up with something soft—silky even. At least that's before you get to the filling, when things get really interesting.

If you fry or bake, the result ends up being decidedly more crispy on the outside. When we choose this route we tend to go for strong, robust flavors inside.

You can, of course, opt not to do any of these things and simply soak your wrapper and, well, wrap. Perfect if the stuffing is a salad or cooked ingredients.

pancake rolls

makes 15 to 20 pancakes

1⅓ cups dried Chinese mushrooms

2 ounces rice vermicelli

1 garlic clove, peeled and finely
    chopped

1 tablespoon finely chopped
    scallion

⅔ cup finely chopped canned
    water chestnuts

1 tablespoon soy sauce

1 tablespoon *mirin* (see page 11)

1 tablespoon toasted sesame oil

1 red chile, finely diced

1 tablespoon fish sauce (*nam pla*)

½ teaspoon light brown sugar

½ cup bean sprouts

1 tablespoon roughly chopped mint

1 tablespoon roughly chopped
    cilantro

3½ ounces Chinese cabbage,
    finely sliced

salt and white pepper

8-inch or 6¼-inch rice paper
    (spring roll) wrappers/skins

chili sauce (see page 22), to serve

In a small heatproof bowl, soak the mushrooms in boiling water for 10 minutes, drain, and finely dice, discarding the tough stems.

Soften the vermicelli according to the instructions on the package, drain, and roughly chop.

Combine the mushrooms and noodles with the remaining filling ingredients and stir thoroughly, seasoning with salt and pepper.

In a medium bowl, soak a rice paper wrapper in warm water until pliable, 1 to 2 minutes, remove, and add another to soak. Place a generous spoonful of the mixture in the center of the paper, and roll up to form a cigar, tucking in the ends as you go. Place seam-side down on a plate and repeat until all the papers and filling are used up. Cover with a damp dishtowel if not serving immediately. Serve with the chili sauce.

If you are using the 8-inch size rice papers, allow 1½ ounces of mixture per roll; if using the 6¼-inch size, allow 1 ounce per roll. If you have an electric set of scales you might consider putting the paper on the scales, setting to zero, and then proceeding with the measured mixture.

shrimp and mango rolls

makes 20 to 25 rolls

1 pound cooked, peeled shrimp
1 mango, pitted, peeled, and diced
grated zest and juice of 1 lime
2 tablespoons fish sauce (*nam pla*)
2 teaspoons light brown sugar
large handful of bean sprouts
small bunch of Thai basil, leaves
    picked and roughly chopped
small bunch of mint, leaves picked
    and roughly chopped
salt and white pepper

20 x 8-inch or 25 x 6¼-inch rice
    paper (spring roll) wrappers/
    skins

In a medium bowl, combine all the filling ingredients, season with salt and pepper, and toss to mix.

In another bowl, soak a rice paper in warm water until pliable, 1 to 2 minutes, remove, and add another to soak. Place a generous spoonful of the mixture in the center of the paper and roll up to form a cigar, tucking in the ends as you go. Place seam-side down on a plate and repeat until all the papers and filling are used up. Cover with a damp dishtowel if not serving immediately.

seafood rolls

makes 30 to 40 pancakes

handful of bean sprouts
2 tablespoons finely diced fennel bulb
1 small head of Bibb lettuce, finely
    shredded
2 tablespoons finely sliced scallion
1¼-inch piece of fresh ginger,
    peeled and grated
2 garlic cloves, peeled and finely
    chopped
1 tablespoon fish sauce (*nam pla*)
1 tablespoon soy sauce
1 teaspoon toasted sesame oil
1 red chile, peeled and finely diced
bunch of cilantro, leaves picked
juice of 1 lime
14 ounces cooked, peeled shrimp
1 pound cooked and picked
    crabmeat (at least 50%
    brown meat)
salt and white pepper

8-inch or 6¼-inch rice paper
(spring roll) wrappers/skins

In a medium bowl, combine all the filling ingredients, season well with salt and pepper, and toss well to mix.

In another bowl, soak a rice paper in warm water until pliable, 1–2 minutes, remove, and add another to soak. Place a generous spoonful of the mixture in the center of the paper and roll up to form a cigar, tucking in the ends as you go. Place seam-side down on a plate and repeat until all the papers and filling are used up. Cover with a damp dishtowel if not serving immediately.

shrimp salad rolls

makes about 8

for the dressing
finely grated zest and juice of
    1 lime
1 teaspoon fish sauce (*nam pla*)
1 teaspoon hoisin sauce
1 chile, seeded and finely sliced
1 garlic clove, peeled and minced

for the rolls
3½ ounces cooked, peeled shrimp
handful of bean sprouts
⅓ cup frozen peas, defrosted
1 medium carrot, peeled and
    julienned
2 tablespoons roughly chopped
    cilantro
2 teaspoons sesame seed, briefly
    toasted in a hot, dry skillet

6¼-inch Vietnamese rice paper
    (spring roll) wrappers/skins
sweet chili dipping sauce (see
    page 16), to serve

In a small bowl, combine all the dressing ingredients and set aside.

In a medium bowl, combine the shrimp, bean sprouts, peas, carrot, cilantro, and sesame seed. Pour over the dressing and mix well.

In another bowl, dip the wrappers one by one in hot water for about 30 seconds. Remove and lay on a board to soften. Place a generous spoonful of the salad mixture in the center of a wrapper, and fold one side of the paper over. Tuck in each end and then roll over to seal the final side. Place seam-side down on a plate and repeat with the other wrappers. Cover with a damp dishtowel if not using immediately.

Transfer the rolls to a large serving plate or divide among individual dishes. Serve with sweet chili sauce, for dipping.

mushroom and chicken gyozas

makes about 60

1 ⅓ cups dried Chinese mushrooms

7 ounces ground chicken

2 garlic cloves, peeled and finely
    chopped

1 ¼-inch piece of fresh ginger,
    peeled and grated

3 ½ ounces Chinese cabbage, finely
    sliced

1 tablespoon soy sauce

1 tablespoon *mirin* (see page 11)

2 tablespoons finely chopped
    scallion

1 tablespoon toasted sesame oil

1 red chile, finely diced

1 tablespoon fish sauce (*nam pla*)

½ teaspoon sugar

⅔ cup finely diced canned
    water chestnuts

salt and white pepper

60 wonton wrappers/skins

vegetable oil, for pan-frying

gyoza sauce (see page 23),
    to serve

In a small heatproof bowl, soak the mushrooms in boiling water for 10 minutes, drain, and finely slice, discarding the tough stems. Add to the rest of the filling ingredients in a medium bowl and mix well. It is best to do this using your hands: as you work, the meat will absorb the liquid. Season well with salt and pepper.

Put a teaspoonful of the mixture in the center of each wonton skin. Moisten the edges with a little water and then fold over to create a half-moon shape. Press down to form a seal.

Heat a large skillet over medium heat until hot and almost smoking, about 1 to 2 minutes, and add 1 tablespoon vegetable oil. Reduce the heat to medium, put 4 to 6 dumplings in the pan, and sauté gently until just starting to brown, 1 minute each side. Don't overcrowd the pan or they will stew.

Remove the pan from the heat, add 3 tablespoons water, and cover immediately with a lid or aluminum foil. Return to the heat for 1 minute, then remove and set aside for another 2 minutes, by which time the *gyozas* will be heated through. Repeat for the remaining *gyozas*. It is quicker if you can use 2 pans, starting to heat the second one just before adding the water to the first pan.

Serve with the *gyoza* sauce. Ideally, serve one batch while you prepare the next because they are best warm.

pork gyozas

makes about 80

5 ounces Chinese cabbage, finely
    chopped
⅓ cup finely chopped canned
    bamboo shoots
1 pound ground pork
1 tablespoon soy sauce
1 tablespoon fish sauce (*nam pla*)
1 tablespoon *mirin* (see page 11)
2 tablespoons finely chopped
    shallots
1¼-inch piece of fresh ginger,
    peeled and grated
1 tablespoon seasame seed,
    briefly toasted in a hot,
    dry skillet
1 tablespoon roughly chopped
    cilantro
½ teaspoon sugar
1 large egg, lightly beaten
1 red chile, seeded and finely
    chopped
salt and white pepper

80 wonton wrappers/skins
vegetable oil, for pan-frying
gyoza sauce (see page 23),
    to serve

In a medium bowl, combine all the ingredients for the filling and mix together. It is best to do this with your hands. Thoroughly season with salt and pepper.

Put a teaspoonful of the mixture in the center of each wonton skin. Moisten the edges with a little water and then fold over to create a half-moon shape. Press down to form a seal.

Heat a large skillet over medium heat until hot and almost smoking, about 1 to 2 minutes, and add 1 tablespoon vegetable oil. Reduce the heat to medium, put 4–6 dumplings in the pan, and sauté gently until just starting to brown, about 1 minute each side. Don't overcrowd the pan or they will stew.

Remove the pan from the heat, add 3 tablespoons water, and cover immediately with a lid or with aluminum foil. Return to the heat for 1 minute, then remove and set aside for another 2 minutes, by which time the *gyozas* will be heated through. Repeat for the remaining *gyozas*. It is quicker if you can use 2 pans, starting to heat the second just before adding the water to the first pan.

Serve with the *gyoza* sauce.

gamama

quick

Fast food takes on a new meaning with noodles. Here you have healthy ingredients. Fresh too. Combined in, at most, 10 minutes. Altogether a different proposition to some fast food we could mention. When you eat a noodle dish at wagamama, the only precooked part is the noodles. After that, what you eat is cooked only when you order it. We like the discipline. We also like the result.

This is why we deliver food when it is cooked. That way we feel you get the best. This is important when you want to eat something nutritious. It also tastes better.

None of the dishes in this book takes that long. Just like in the restaurants, the aim is really to get food on the table in a matter of minutes rather than hours. This chapter, however, contains the super-charged recipes. Those that come at you so that you are caught unaware. Supper in seconds you might say.

It might not seem that fast as you chop away with no heat in sight. But this is the way with noodles. A hot wok will wilt bok choy in moments, seal chicken in seconds, render a scallop a deeply golden caramelized color in no time. Well, very little time.

The secret to this really fast noodle cooking lies in choosing ingredients that need very little heat to give their best and which are suitably cut. So take care on the board.

There are often times when we want food fast. Not always, but certainly occasionally. There is every reason why the care taken should be just the same as with more complicated dishes. Good food fast? Why not?

serves 2

½ cup unsalted peanuts
3½ ounces medium egg noodles

for the dressing
1 to 2 red chiles (or to taste),
    seeded and finely chopped
4 Chinese flowering chives (see
    page 11), finely chopped
2 teaspoons rice vinegar
finely grated zest and juice of
    ½ lemon

2 tablespoons vegetable oil
1 red onion, peeled and chopped
1 garlic clove, peeled and crushed
1 red bell pepper, seeded and
    thinly sliced
1 cup sliced zucchini
handful of baby spinach
salt and white pepper

chive and chile noodles

Preheat the oven to 400°F. Roast the peanuts on a baking sheet until just colored, 5 to 6 minutes. Transfer to a cold plate and let cool. Roughly chop.

Cook the noodles according to the instructions on the package, drain, and refresh under cold water.

Make the dressing: Whisk together the chiles, chives, rice vinegar, and lemon zest and juice. Set aside.

In a hot wok, heat the vegetable oil and stir-fry the onion until softened, 2 to 3 minutes. Add the garlic, red bell pepper, and zucchini, and stir-fry over medium heat until lightly browned, another 4 minutes. Add the peanuts and cook for another minute.

Add the noodles and spinach and toss through the vegetables until the noodles are hot and the spinach just wilted. Add the dressing and ensure that all ingredients are evenly coated. Check the seasoning and serve.

spinach and soba noodles

serves 2

3½ ounces *soba* noodles

1 tablespoon vegetable oil

3 garlic cloves, peeled and mashed

1¼-inch piece of fresh ginger,
    peeled and grated

½ pound baby spinach

1 tablespoon oyster sauce

1 tablespoon toasted sesame oil

juice of 1 lime

2 teaspoons sesame seed, briefly
    toasted in a hot, dry skillet

1 chile, seeded and finely
    chopped

Cook the noodles according to the instructions on the package, drain, and refresh under cold water.

In a hot wok, heat the oil and stir-fry the garlic, ginger, and spinach for 2 minutes. Add the noodles, toss once, remove from the heat, and stir in the oyster sauce and sesame oil.

Squeeze over the lime juice and serve with the sesame seed and chile scattered over the top.

spiced vegetable noodles

serves 2

3½ ounces thin rice vermicelli

1 tablespoon vegetable oil

2 garlic cloves, peeled and finely
    chopped

1¼-inch piece of fresh ginger,
    peeled and grated

2 lemongrass stalks, outer leaves
    removed, finely chopped

1 tablespoon finely chopped
    shallots

2 red chiles, finely chopped

1 teaspoon curry powder

handful of finely sliced Bibb lettuce

1 cucumber, seeded and cut
    into batons

handful of snow peas, sliced
    lengthwise

1 tablespoon soy sauce

scant ½ teaspoon brown sugar

salt and white pepper

Cook the vermicelli according to the instructions on the package, drain, and refresh under cold water.

In a hot wok, heat the vegetable oil and stir-fry the garlic, ginger, lemongrass, shallots, and chiles for 1 minute. Add the curry powder, lettuce, cucumber, and snow peas, and stir-fry until the vegetables are cooked, but still crunchy, about 5 minutes.

Add the soy sauce, sugar, and noodles and toss so that everything is well coated. Season with salt and pepper and serve.

red bell pepper and bok choy with spiced udon noodles

serves 2

5 ounces *udon* noodles

2 garlic cloves, peeled and minced

1 tablespoon dried shrimp, soaked in hot water, drained, and chopped

1¼-inch piece of fresh ginger, peeled and sliced

2 lemongrass stalks, outer leaves removed, finely chopped

1 tablespoon finely chopped red onion

bunch of cilantro

3 tablespoons vegetable oil

1 red bell pepper, seeded and very thinly sliced

1 head of bok choy, roughly chopped

salt and white pepper

1–2 chiles (or to taste), finely chopped

Cook the noodles according to the instructions on the package, drain, and refresh under cold water.

Combine all the other ingredients except the oil, red bell pepper, bok choy, and chile in a pestle and mortar and grind to a paste. Stir in 2 tablespoons of the oil.

In a hot wok, heat the remaining tablespoon oil, add the prepared paste, and stir-fry until it loses its raw flavor, about 2 minutes. Add the vegetables and carry on cooking for another 2 minutes. Add the noodles to the wok and toss so that everything is well coated.

Check the seasoning and serve sprinkled with the chile.

quick vegetable noodles

serves 2

3½ ounces flat egg noodles

1 tablespoon vegetable oil

2 chiles, seeded and finely diced

2 garlic cloves, peeled and finely chopped

1¼-inch piece of fresh ginger, peeled and grated

1 red onion, peeled and cut vertically into eighths

3½ ounces string beans, trimmed and sliced into 2½-inch lengths

1 red bell pepper, seeded and sliced lengthwise

1 tablespoon soy sauce

2 tablespoons sake

1 teaspoon brown sugar

1 tablespoon oyster sauce

Cook the noodles according to the instructions on the package, drain, and refresh under cold water.

In a hot wok, heat the oil and stir-fry the chiles, garlic, and ginger for 30 seconds. Add the vegetables and continue to stir-fry until wilted, about 5 to 6 minutes, adding 1 tablespoon water halfway through. Stir in the soy sauce, sake, sugar, and oyster sauce along with the noodles. Toss so that everything is well coated and heated through, and serve.

chili prawns with soba noodles

5 ounces *soba* noodles

1 teaspoon toasted sesame oil

2 tablespoons rice vinegar

1 tablespoon soy sauce

2 teaspoons light brown sugar

scant teaspoon Chinese chili paste
(available from Asian markets)

1 tablespoon vegetable oil

½ pound raw, peeled shrimp,
deveined and roughly chopped

2 scallions, finely sliced

1¼-inch piece of fresh ginger,
peeled and finely chopped

1 garlic clove, peeled and crushed

few cilantro leaves

Cook the noodles according to the instructions on the package, drain, then return to the pot and toss with the sesame oil.

In a small bowl, combine the rice vinegar, soy sauce, sugar, and chili paste.

In a hot wok, heat the oil and stir-fry the shrimp, scallions, ginger, and garlic for 1 to 2 minutes.

Add the chili mixture to the wok and cook for 1 minute. Add the noodles and toss so that everything is well coated and heated through. Scatter over the cilantro.

spiced scallops with spinach, mint, and sweet chili dressing

serves 2

2½ ounces *udon* noodles

1 tablespoon vegetable oil

1¼-inch piece of fresh ginger, peeled and grated

2 garlic cloves, peeled and minced with a little salt

pinch of Chinese five-spice powder

1 tablespoon black bean sauce

6 to 8 sea scallops, shelled and trimmed

2 handfuls of baby spinach

bunch of mint, leaves picked

3 tablespoons chicken stock (see page 13)

1 tablespoon soy sauce

pinch of sugar

salt and white pepper

2 teaspoons toasted sesame oil

2 teaspoons sweet chili dipping sauce (see page 16)

2 scallions, finely sliced

Cook the noodles according to the instructions on the package, drain, and refresh under cold water.

In a hot wok, heat the vegetable oil and stir-fry the ginger, garlic, five-spice, black bean sauce, and scallops for 2 minutes. Add the spinach and mint leaves, stock, soy sauce, sugar, and sesame oil and simmer until reduced slightly, about 1 minute. Check the seasoning. Add the noodles and toss everything so that it is well coated and heated through.

Serve drizzled with the sweet chili dipping sauce and topped with the scallions.

3½ ounces flat Chinese noodles
5 dried shiitake mushrooms
1 tablespoon vegetable oil
1 onion, peeled and finely chopped
1 carrot, peeled and thinly sliced
2 garlic cloves, peeled and crushed
1¼-inch piece of fresh ginger,
    peeled and grated
7 ounces skinless salmon fillet, cut
    into 1¼-inch squares
2 tablespoons soy sauce
⅓ cup chicken stock (see page 13)
2 teaspoons cornstarch, dissolved
    in 2 tablespoons water
salt and white pepper

soy-braised salmon

Cook the noodles according to the instructions on the package, drain, and refresh under cold water. Soak the mushrooms in ½ cup boiling water.

In a hot wok, heat the oil and stir-fry the onion, carrot, garlic, ginger, and salmon for 1 minute. Add the soy sauce, cover, turn the heat down, and simmer for 2 minutes.

Drain the mushrooms, reserving the liquid. Remove and discard the tough stems and finely slice. Add the chicken stock to the pan with the mushrooms, reserved liquid, and dissolved cornstarch. Bring to a boil and add the noodles, tossing to combine and taking care not to break up the salmon too much. Taste and season with salt and pepper, then serve.

serves 2

for the marinade
1 tablespoon soy sauce
1 tablespoon sake
2 garlic cloves, peeled and minced
1¼-inch piece of fresh ginger,
    peeled and grated

3½ ounces somen noodles
1 tablespoon vegetable oil
3½ ounces skinless salmon fillet or
    cutlets, cut into bite-size pieces
2 heads of bok choy, quartered
    lengthwise
1 teaspoon cornstarch mixed with
    a little cold water
2 tablespoons soy sauce
2½ cups chicken stock (see
    page 13)
2 tablespoons sake

salmon and bok choy noodles

Make the marinade: In a medium bowl, combine the marinade ingredients, add the salmon, and toss gently so that the pieces are well coated. Cover and set aside for 1 hour; overnight in the fridge is even better.

Cook the noodles according to the instructions on the package, drain, and refresh under cold water.

In a hot wok, heat the oil and stir-fry the salmon and bok choy for 2 minutes. Blend the cornstarch paste with the soy sauce and add to the wok with the chicken stock and sake. Simmer until everything has thickened and the fish is cooked, about 3 to 4 minutes.

Toss the noodles through and serve.

serves 2

3½ ounces medium egg noodles

1 teaspoon cornstarch

1 tablespoon soy sauce

2 tablespoons vegetable oil

5 ounces dark chicken meat
  (leg or thigh), cut into bite-
  size pieces

1 green bell pepper, seeded and
  cut into 1¼-inch pieces

2 tablespoons fermented black
  beans, rinsed and roughly
  chopped

4 garlic cloves, peeled and finely
  chopped

1¼-inch piece of fresh ginger,
  peeled and minced

1 chili, seeded and finely
  chopped

2½ cups chicken stock (see
  page 13)

1 tablespoon sake

chicken and egg noodles with black bean sauce

Cook the noodles according to the instructions on the package, drain, and refresh under cold water.

Blend the cornstarch with the soy sauce.

Heat a wok and when hot add the vegetable oil. Add the chicken and green bell pepper and stir-fry for 2 minutes. Add the black beans, garlic, ginger, and chile and continue cooking until the chicken has almost cooked, another 3 to 4 minutes.

Stir in the chicken stock, blended cornstarch, and sake. Simmer for 2 minutes.

Spoon the noodles onto 2 plates, and serve topped with the chicken and black bean sauce.

serves 2

3½ ounces *soba* noodles

2 cups chicken stock (see page 13)

1 leek, white part only, thinly sliced

2 tablespoons soy sauce

2 teaspoons fish sauce (*nam pla*)

1 tablespoon sake

5 ounces boneless, skinless chicken
  breast, cut into bite-size pieces

2 handfuls of baby spinach leaves,
  roughly chopped

2 teaspoons sesame seed, briefly
  toasted in a hot, dry skillet

chicken, spinach, and soba noodle soup

Cook the noodles according to the instructions on the package, drain, and refresh under cold water.

In a saucepan, bring the chicken stock to a boil and add the leek, soy sauce, fish sauce, and sake. Cook until the leek softens, about 10 minutes. Turn the heat down, add the chicken, and poach gently until cooked, about 4 to 5 minutes. Add the spinach, bring back to a boil, and remove from the heat.

Divide the noodles equally between 2 bowls and ladle over the spinach, chicken, and broth. Sprinkle with the sesame seed and serve.

stir-fried chicken noodles

for the marinade

2 tablespoons soy sauce

2 tablespoons *mirin* (see page 11)

1 teaspoon sugar

3½ ounces chicken thigh meat, cut
     into bite-size pieces

salt and white pepper

3½ ounces medium egg noodles

1 tablespoon vegetable oil

2 garlic cloves, peeled and finely
     chopped

½ red bell pepper, seeded and
     finely sliced

handful of snow peas, thinly sliced
     lengthwise

2 teaspoons toasted sesame oil

2 teaspoons sesame seed, briefly
     toasted in a hot, dry skillet

bunch of cilantro, leaves picked

In a medium bowl, combine the marinade ingredients. Add the chicken, and toss well to coat the pieces. Season with salt and pepper, cover, and set aside for 1 hour; overnight in the fridge is even better.

Drain the chicken, reserving the marinade.

Cook the noodles according to the instructions on the package, drain, and refresh under cold water.

In a hot wok, heat the vegetable oil and stir-fry the garlic for 30 seconds. Add the chicken and stir-fry for 2 minutes, then add the red bell pepper, snow peas, and reserved marinade and stir-fry for another 2 minutes. Add the noodles and sesame oil and toss so that everything is well coated and heated through. Check the seasoning.

Serve with a sprinkling of the sesame seed and cilantro.

chicken fried noodles with sausage

serves 2

3½ ounces Thai-style rice noodles

2 tablespoons vegetable oil

1 large egg, beaten and seasoned

2 garlic cloves, peeled and finely chopped

1 red chile, seeded and finely chopped

3½ ounces boneless, skinless chicken breast, cut into bite-size pieces

2 ounces firm pork sausage, sliced

1 head of bok choy, roughly sliced lengthwise

1 teaspoon brown sugar

1 tablespoon soy sauce

handful of bean sprouts

2½ ounces *kamaboko-aka* (see page 11), sliced

2 scallions, finely sliced

Cook the noodles according to the instructions on the package, drain, and refresh under cold water.

Put 1 tablespoon of the vegetable oil into a hot wok. Add the egg, swirl so that it coats the bottom, and cook for 1 minute. Remove, let cool, then roll up and thinly slice.

Add the remaining tablespoon oil to the wok and stir-fry the garlic and chile for 30 seconds. Add the chicken, sausage, and bok choy. Stir-fry until the chicken is cooked, about 3 to 4 minutes.

Add the sugar, soy sauce, bean sprouts, and *kamaboko-aka* along with the reserved noodles and the egg, and toss so that everything is heated through.

Serve topped with the scallions.

stir-fried chicken and mushrooms with somen noodles

serves 2

3½ ounces *somen* noodles

1 tablespoon vegetable oil

2 boneless, skinless chicken breasts, cut into bite-size slices

1 cup thinly sliced button mushrooms

1 heaping cup thinly sliced shiitake mushrooms

1¼-inch piece of fresh ginger, peeled and grated

2 garlic cloves, peeled and mashed

2 teaspoons soy sauce

1 tablespoon sake

1 tablespoon *mirin* (see page 11)

1 lime, cut into wedges

handful of cilantro leaves

Cook the noodles according to the instructions on the package, drain, and refresh under cold water.

In a hot wok, heat the oil over a medium heat and stir-fry the chicken, mushrooms, ginger, and garlic for 2 to 3 minutes. Add the soy sauce, sake, *mirin,* and 2 tablespoons water and continue to stir-fry until the chicken is cooked, about 2 minutes.

Stir in the noodles to heat through and serve with a wedge of lime and a scattering of cilantro leaves.

pork and soba noodles

serves 2

7 ounces pork tenderloin, thinly
    sliced
1 tablespoon *char siu* sauce
    (Chinese barbecue sauce,
    widely available)
½ teaspoon Chinese five-spice
    powder
¼ teaspoon ground cinnamon
2 tablespoons sake
3½ ounces thick *soba* noodles
1 tablespoon vegetable oil
2½ ounces flowering greens (*choy
    sum*)
¾ cup sliced button mushrooms
handful of bean sprouts
½ red bell pepper, seeded and
    finely sliced
2 scallions, finely sliced
2 tablespoons *yasai soba* dressing
    (see page 16)
2 large eggs, lightly beaten
1 tablespoon finely sliced *kimchee*
    (see page 11)
2 teaspoons sesame seed

In a plastic food bag, combine the pork, *char siu* sauce, Chinese five-spice, cinnamon, and sake and leave in the fridge overnight to marinate.

Cook the noodles according to the instructions on the package, drain, and refresh under cold water.

In a hot wok, heat the oil and add, one at a time, the noodles, pork, flowering greens, mushrooms, bean sprouts, red bell pepper, scallions, *yasai soba* dressing, and eggs, tossing well and stir-frying for a total of 6 to 7 minutes.

Serve sprinkled with the *kimchee* and sesame seed.

This recipe was created by Geraldo Suwu, from wagamama in Amsterdam.

stir-fried beef with broccoli

serves 2

5 ounces medium egg noodles
1½ cups small broccoli florets
2 tablespoons vegetable oil
5 ounces beef (boneless top loin
    steak), thinly sliced into
    bite-size pieces
2 garlic cloves, peeled and mashed
1¼-inch piece of fresh ginger,
    peeled and grated
1 tablespoon soy sauce
1 tablespoon fish sauce (*nam pla*)
salt and white pepper

Cook the noodles according to the instructions on the package, drain, and refresh under cold water.

In a saucepan, blanch the broccoli in boiling salted water, 2 to 3 minutes, drain, and refresh under cold water.

In a hot wok, heat the oil over medium heat and stir-fry the beef, garlic, and ginger until the beef is almost cooked, about 3 to 4 minutes. Add the noodles, broccoli, soy sauce, and fish sauce. Toss so that everything is well combined and heated through.

Check the seasoning and serve.

sweet and sour beef noodles

serves 2

3½ ounces medium egg noodles
1 tablespoon vegetable oil
2 garlic cloves, peeled and finely
    chopped
1¼-inch piece of fresh ginger,
    peeled and finely chopped
5 ounces beef (boneless top
    loin steak is probably best),
    cut into thin strips
½ red bell pepper, seeded and
    finely sliced
2 teaspoons cornstarch
2 tablespoons soy sauce
1 teaspoon sugar
⅓ cup chicken stock (see page 13)
1 tablespoon *mirin* (see page 11)
1 tablespoon rice vinegar
juice of 1 lime
2 tablespoons frozen peas,
    defrosted
handful of bean sprouts
bunch of cilantro, leaves picked
2 scallions, finely sliced

Cook the noodles according to the instructions on the package, drain, and refresh under cold water.

In a hot wok, heat the oil and stir-fry the garlic and ginger for 30 seconds. Add the beef, toss well, and then add the red bell pepper, stir-frying for 3 minutes. Blend the cornstarch with the soy sauce and add, along with the sugar, chicken stock, *mirin,* and rice vinegar. Toss so that everything is well coated and simmer to thicken slightly, about 1 minute. Add the noodles, lime juice, peas, and beansprouts. Cook everything for another 3 minutes.

Serve scattered with the cilantro and scallions.

IM SUM AND DONE!

OU HAVE

- Frozen pot stickers
- Frozen shrimp
- Frozen edamame
- Cocktail sauce

FRIENDS BRING

- ☐ Broccoli slaw
- ☐ Pineapple juice
- ☐ Cilantro
- ☐ Scallions

---

ot Stickers with Sesame-Soy ipping Sauce

cup soy sauce • 2 tbsp. rice negar • 2 tsp. sugar • 1 tsp. toasted same oil • 1 scallion, thinly sliced : lb. frozen pot stickers (any variety) resh cilantro, for garnish → In small wl, whisk soy sauce, rice vinegar, gar and 2 tbsp. water until sugar solves. Mix in sesame oil and allion. Prepare pot stickers per ckage directions; arrange on latter. Serve with dipping sauce d garnish with cilantro. Serves 8.

'S #1

RGER

VE IT

entertaining

Entertaining with noodles really is a doddle. No complicated cooking, just good clean flavors. The preparation is easy, the cooking is quick and hassle-free, and the serving amounts to little more than a few bowls. You can get your friends to help or do it all beforehand—nothing could be simpler. Any cooking is done at the last minute, which means you remain in control.

Noodle stalls in Asia are based on the same principle: advance preparation = speed of service. You chop, precook the noodles, and hold. Wait for everyone to arrive and then magically it all appears. The secret lies in doing enough, but not too much. Nobody wants to reheat things when stir-frying is so quick.

Sharing food is such an important part of entertaining and these kinds of dishes are perfect for communal eating. A lettuce leaf stuffed with scallops and noodles to start perhaps, and then, when you sit down, salmon teriyaki with *soba* noodle salad, or Thai-style shrimp with peanuts and chile, or beef and black bean sauce with egg noodles.

A salad or two might bring everything to a refreshing conclusion. Offer a summer salad with pickled ginger (*gari*) on warm days, or marinated mushroom salad with cellophane noodles for when the weather is a bit more inclement.

This is cooking to be done out in front of your guests, cooking to be proud of, cooking to be enjoyed with the minimum of fuss and the maximum of taste, texture, and flavor. Fast food of the right kind.

stuffed lettuce leaves with scallops, noodles, and soy dipping sauce

2 ounces rice vermicelli, broken into
    2½-inch lengths
vegetable oil
12 sea scallops, shelled, trimmed,
    and sliced in half horizontally
1 garlic clove, peeled and mashed
1¼-inch piece of fresh ginger,
    peeled and grated
1 tablespoon soy sauce
1 tablespoon hoisin sauce
salt and white pepper
12 Bibb lettuce leaves
½ cucumber, seeded and cut
    into matchsticks
handful of bean sprouts
1 tablespoon crispy fried shallots
    (available from Asian markets),
    optional
lime wedges
soy dipping sauce (see page 22)

Cook the vermicelli according to the instructions on the package, drain, and refresh under cold water.

In a hot wok, heat a little oil and stir-fry the scallops until they just color, about 2 minutes. Add the garlic and ginger and stir-fry for another minute. Add the soy and hoisin sauces and the drained noodles. Season with salt and pepper and remove from the heat.

To serve, arrange the lettuce leaves on a large plate. Place 2 scallop halves in each lettuce leaf along with some noodles. Top with the cucumber and bean sprouts, crispy fried shallots, and a wedge of lime for squeezing.

Serve with the soy dipping sauce on the side.

green curry noodles

3½ ounces egg noodles
2 tablespoons vegetable oil
handful of baby corn
1 red bell pepper, seeded and cut
    into strips
1 small head of broccoli, broken
    into florets
1 heaping tablespoon green curry
    paste (see page 18)
7 ounces (about 1 heaping cup)
    canned bamboo shoots,
    drained and rinsed
handful of snow peas
salt and white pepper
handful of cilantro leaves

Cook the noodles according to the instructions on the package, drain, and refresh under cold water.

In a hot wok, heat the oil and stir-fry the baby corn, red bell pepper, and broccoli until they just start to color, about 5 minutes. Add the green curry paste and cook until it loses its raw flavor, about another minute. Add the coconut milk and ½ cup water, together with the bamboo shoots and snow peas. Cook for 2 minutes.

Add the noodles to the wok and toss them thoroughly so that everything is well combined.

Check the seasoning and serve sprinkled with the cilantro leaves.

somen noodle shrimp with sweet ginger dip

serves 3 to 4

for the sweet ginger dip
2 tablespoons soy sauce
1 teaspoon fish sauce (*nam pla*)
1 tablespoon sugar
1¼-inch piece of fresh ginger,
    peeled and grated

3½ ounces *somen* noodles, broken
    into 2½-inch lengths
12 raw shrimp, peeled but tail
    on, deveined, and seasoned
1 sheet of *nori* seaweed, cut into
    12 strips, 3½ inches long
vegetable oil, for deep-frying

bamboo skewers

Make the dip: In a saucepan, combine the soy sauce, fish sauce, sugar, and ginger, bring to a boil and simmer until just thickening, about 3 minutes. Strain and let cool.

In a medium heatproof bowl, cover the noodles with boiling water and soak for 2 minutes, drain thoroughly, and pat dry with a clean dishtowel.

Push a skewer down each shrimp from the tail end toward the head. Place a strip of seaweed on a board. Lay a pinch of noodles about the same width as the shrimp at right angles to the seaweed. Place a skewered shrimp on top of the noodles. Moisten the visible part of the seaweed and roll up to seal so that it forms a band around the noodles and shrimp. Repeat with each shrimp.

Pour the oil to a depth of 1½ inches in a suitable pan. Heat over medium-high heat. When hot, drop in the shrimp in batches and cook, turning occasionally, until the noodles are crispy and golden brown, about 3 minutes.

Drain on paper towels and serve with the sweet ginger dip.

thai-style shrimp with peanuts and chili

serves 2

3½ ounces wide Thai-style rice
    noodles
2 tablespoons vegetable oil
1 tablespoon red curry paste
    (see page 16)
12 raw, peeled shrimp, deveined
2 garlic cloves, peeled and crushed
2 small heads of bok choy, sliced
    lengthwise
handful of frozen peas, defrosted
6 baby corn
small bunch of cilantro, stems
    finely chopped, leaves reserved
⅓ cup soy milk
juice of 1 lime
1 tablespoon fish sauce (*nam pla*)
2 teaspoons light brown sugar
salt and white pepper
1 tablespoon roasted peanuts

Cook the noodles according to the instructions on the package, drain, and refresh under cold water.

In a wok, heat the vegetable oil and when hot add the curry paste. Stir-fry for 2 minutes, and then add the shrimp and garlic. Cook until the shrimp start to lose their raw color, about 4 minutes. Transfer to a bowl and set aside.

Add the bok choy, peas, baby corn, and cilantro stems to the wok, and stir-fry until the vegetables start to wilt and color, about 3 to 4 minutes.

Return the shrimp mixture to the pan, along with the soy milk, lime juice, fish sauce, and sugar. Season with salt and pepper, add the noodles, and cook for 3 to 4 minutes.

Serve with a scattering of peanuts and reserved cilantro leaves.

salmon teriyaki with udon noodle salad

serves 2

2 salmon fillets, skin on
3 tablespoons soy sauce
3 tablespoons *mirin* (see page 11)
5 ounces *udon* noodles
1 red chile (or to taste), finely
    chopped
2 scallions, finely chopped
large handful of baby spinach leaves
bunch of cilantro, leaves picked
    and stems finely chopped
1 tablespoon vegetable oil
2 teaspoons sesame seed, briefly
    toasted in a hot, dry skillet
1 lime
sweet chili dipping sauce (see
    page 16)

for the dressing
2 teaspoons toasted sesame oil
2 teaspoons dark soy sauce
juice of 1 lime

In a shallow bowl, combine the salmon, soy sauce, and *mirin*, toss so that they are well coated, and marinate for 2 hours; overnight in the fridge is even better.

Cook the noodles according to the instructions on the package, drain, and refresh briefly under cold water; they still want to be warm.

In a large bowl, combine the dressing ingredients and toss the noodles through. Add the chile, scallions, spinach, and cilantro, and toss well. Divide between 2 plates.

Heat the vegetable oil in a skillet. Remove the salmon from the marinade, season with salt and pepper, and sear, skin-side down, for 2 minutes. Turn over and fry on the other side for 2 minutes. Turn back onto the skin side and cook until the skin is crisp, another 2 minutes.

Place the salmon (skin-side up) on the noodles, top with the sesame seed, and serve with half a lime and the chili dipping sauce.

monkfish and cilantro with chinese noodles

serves 2

for the marinade

1 teaspoon cornstarch

1 ¼-inch piece of fresh ginger, peeled and grated

2 garlic cloves, peeled and grated

2 teaspoons soy sauce

2 teaspoons oyster sauce

1 tablespoon vegetable oil

7 ounces monkfish fillet, cut into pieces 1 ½ inches long, ¾ inch thick

salt and white pepper

3 ½ ounces medium egg noodles

1 tablespoon vegetable oil

1 teaspoon cornstarch

1 teaspoon soy sauce

pinch of light brown sugar

1 teaspoon oyster sauce

1 teaspoon toasted sesame oil

3 tablespoons chicken stock (see page 13)

large bunch of cilantro, stems trimmed at the base but otherwise intact

1 tablespoon finely sliced scallion

In a medium bowl, combine the marinade ingredients, then add the monkfish pieces, tossing to coat thoroughly. Add a seasoning of salt and pepper. Cover and set aside for 1 hour; overnight in the fridge is even better.

Cook the noodles according to the instructions on the package, drain, and refresh under cold water.

In a hot wok, heat the vegetable oil and stir-fry the monkfish and its marinade until the fish is cooked, about 3 to 4 minutes. Blend the cornstarch with the soy sauce, sugar, and oyster sauce. Add to the wok with the sesame oil and chicken stock and simmer for 30 seconds. Add the cilantro and continue cooking until it wilts, about another 30 seconds. Add the noodles and toss so that everything is combined and heated through. Remove from the heat, and check the seasoning.

Serve sprinkled with the scallion.

Cilantro is undoubtedly a strong herb, but there are times when using it to excess really pays off. Here it is used almost like a vegetable.

1 tablespoon soy sauce
1 garlic clove, peeled and minced
2 teaspoons honey
1 tablespoon *mirin* (see page 11)
1 teaspoon fish sauce (*nam pla*)
2 teaspoons lime juice

2 quail, butterflied (see note
    below)
4½ ounces fresh egg noodles
    (or 3 ounces dried)
3 tablespoons vegetable oil
1 cup sliced portobello mushrooms
¾ cup snow peas
8 baby corn, halved lengthwise
1¼-inch piece of fresh ginger,
    peeled and grated
2 teaspoons soy sauce
2 teaspoons cornstarch
⅓ cup chicken stock (see
    page 13)
1 tablespoon oyster sauce
1 tablespoon *mirin* (see page 11)

marinated quail with stir-fried noodles

In a large bowl, combine the marinade ingredients and stir gently but thoroughly to blend everything. Add the quail and coat thoroughly.

Cook the noodles according to the instructions on the package, drain, and refresh under cold water.

In a hot wok, heat the vegetable oil. Brush the marinade off the quail (reserving the marinade), and sear over medium–low heat (too hot and you will burn the marinade) until well colored and cooked through, about 5 to 6 minutes each side. Remove from the wok and keep warm. Wipe out the wok, add the reserved marinade, the mushrooms, snow peas, baby corn, and ginger and stir-fry for 2 to 3 minutes over high heat.

Combine the soy sauce and cornstarch. Add to the wok with the remaining ingredients, stirring to avoid lumps forming. Once everything starts to bubble, add the noodles and toss to ensure that everything is well coated.

Transfer to a serving dish, top with the quail, and serve.

Butterfly the quail by cutting down either side of the backbone, which should be discarded. Place the quail, breast-side up, on a board and press down firmly to flatten—you need to break the breastbone so that the birds stay flat.

chicken and shrimp hot-pot

serves 4

12 raw, peeled shrimp, deveined

5 ounces dark chicken meat (leg or thigh), roughly chopped

6 shiitake mushrooms, stems removed, roughly chopped

5 Chinese cabbage leaves, sliced

1 carrot, peeled and julienned

2 heads of baby bok choy, roughly chopped

handful of snow peas, trimmed

1¼-inch piece of fresh ginger, peeled and grated

7 ounces *udon* noodles

1 quart chicken stock (see page 13)

1 tablespoon soy sauce

1 tablespoon *mirin* (see page 11)

salt and white pepper

2 scallions, finely sliced

In a casserole dish just large enough to take all the ingredients, arrange the shrimp, chicken, mushrooms, cabbage leaves, carrots, bok choy, snow peas and ginger. Place the noodles on top.

In a saucepan, bring the stock to a boil, add the soy sauce and *mirin*, and season with salt and pepper. Pour the stock over the ingredients and bring to a slow boil over medium heat. Let simmer until all the ingredients are cooked, about 5 minutes.

Let rest for 2 minutes and serve from the casserole dish, sprinkled with the scallions.

crispy chicken noodles

serves 2

3½ ounces medium egg noodles
1¼ cups plus 2 tablespoons
    vegetable oil
1 tablespoon red curry paste
    (see page 16)
3½ ounces dark chicken meat (leg
    or thigh), coarsely chopped
2 heads of bok choy, halved
    lengthwise
small bunch of cilantro, stems
    fincly chopped, leaves reserved
1 tablespoon chopped shallots
salt and white pepper
⅓ cup chicken stock (see
    page 13)
½ cup coconut milk
2 teaspoons fish sauce (*nam pla*)
2 handfuls of bean sprouts
1 red chile, thinly sliced
1 tablespoon mint leaves
juice of 1 lime

Cook the noodles according to the instructions on the package, drain, and refresh under cold water. Add 1 tablespoon of the oil and toss to mix.

In a small saucepan or wok, heat the 1¼ cups oil until it is hot enough to make a piece of noodle fluff up. Working in small batches, cook the noodles until crispy, drain on paper towels, and transfer to 2 plates.

In a hot wok, heat the remaining tablespoon oil. Add the red curry paste, and stir-fry until it loses its raw aroma, about 30 seconds (do not allow it to catch and burn). Add the chicken, bok choy, cilantro stems, and shallots, season with salt, and stir-fry for 3 minutes. Add the chicken stock, bring to a boil, lower the heat, and add the coconut milk and fish sauce. Simmer until the meat is cooked, about 10 minutes. Check the seasoning.

In a medium bowl, combine the bean sprouts, chile, mint, and reserved cilantro leaves and mix well.

To serve, spoon the chicken mixture on top of the crispy noodles, top with the bean sprout mixture, and drizzle with the lime juice.

stir-fried duck with soba noodles, peas, and mint

serves 2

4½ ounces *soba* noodles
1 tablespoon vegetable oil
7 ounces boneless duck breast, skinned and thinly sliced
salt and white pepper
2 garlic cloves, peeled and thinly sliced
2 tablespoons frozen peas, defrosted
3 tablespoons *mirin* (see page 11)
2 tablespoons soy sauce
1 tablespoon canned bamboo shoots, drained
bunch of mint, leaves picked

Cook the noodles according to the instructions on the package, drain, and refresh under cold water.

In a hot wok, heat the oil, season the duck with salt and pepper, and stir-fry until the meat is cooked, about 3 to 4 minutes.

Add the garlic, peas, *mirin*, and soy sauce and continue to stir-fry until everything looks glossy and reduced, about another minute. Add the noodles and toss to ensure that everything is well combined. Taste and adjust the seasoning.

Divide between 2 bowls and serve scattered with the bamboo shoots and mint.

hot and sour pork and shrimp with ramen noodles

serves 2

4½ ounces *ramen* noodles
1 tablespoon vegetable oil
4½ ounces ground pork
6 button mushrooms, sliced
bunch of scallions, cut into 2½-inch lengths
3½ ounces raw, peeled shrimp, deveined
2 red chiles, seeded and finely sliced
2 garlic cloves, peeled and minced with a little salt
2 teaspoons dark brown sugar
1 tablespoon fish sauce (*nam pla*)
1 tablespoon rice vinegar
2 handfuls of bean sprouts
2 tablespoons roughly chopped cilantro leaves
1 lime, halved

Cook the noodles according to the instructions on the package, drain, and refresh under cold water.

In a hot wok, heat the oil and stir-fry the pork for 3 minutes, then add the mushrooms, scallions, shrimp, chiles, garlic, sugar, fish sauce, and rice vinegar. Stir-fry for another 3 minutes.

Add the noodles and toss to ensure that everything is well combined.

Divide between 2 bowls and serve topped with the bean sprouts and cilantro and a lime half to squeeze over.

beef and black bean sauce with egg noodles

serves 2

4½ ounces medium egg noodles

1 tablespoon vegetable oil, plus
    extra for the noodles

2 teaspoons cornstarch

⅓ cup chicken stock (see page 13)

1 red onion, peeled and cut
    vertically into eighths

1 green bell pepper, seeded and
    cut into 1½-inch squares

3½ ounces beef (boneless top loin
    steak), finely sliced

2 garlic cloves, peeled and
    thinly sliced

1½-inch piece of fresh ginger,
    peeled and finely grated

1 tablespoon black bean sauce

1 red chile, seeded and finely sliced

salt and white pepper

Cook the noodles according to the instructions on the package, drain, and refresh under cold water. Toss with a little oil.

Dissolve the cornstarch in 2 tablespoons of the chicken stock.

In a hot wok, heat the oil and stir-fry the red onion and green bell pepper for 4 minutes. Add the beef, garlic, and ginger and continue to stir-fry for 1 minute. Add the black bean sauce, chile, chicken stock, and dissolved cornstarch. Stir until the sauce thickens, about 1 minute. Taste and adjust the seasoning.

Divide the noodles between 2 bowls. Pour over the beef mixture and serve.

five-spice beef with rice noodles

serves 2

for the marinade

½ teaspoon Chinese five-spice
    powder

2 teaspoons oyster sauce

2 teaspoons soy sauce

1 tablespoon *mirin* (see page 11)

1 teaspoon cornstarch

7 ounces beef (boneless top loin
    steak), thinly sliced

5 ounces flat Thai-style rice noodles

2 teaspoons vegetable oil

1¼-inch piece of fresh ginger,
    peeled and finely chopped

2 garlic cloves, finely chopped

1 red bell pepper, seeded and cut
    into strips

2 teaspoons soy sauce

⅓ cup chicken stock (see page 13)

salt and white pepper

2 scallions, finely sliced

In a large bowl, combine the marinade ingredients. Add the steak and stir to coat thoroughly. Cover and set aside for at least 1 hour; overnight in the fridge is even better.

Cook the noodles according to the instructions on the package, drain, and refresh under cold water.

In a hot wok, heat the oil and stir-fry the ginger, garlic, and red bell pepper for 2 minutes.

Add the beef, reserving the marinade. Stir-fry until just cooked, about 2 minutes. Add the marinade along with the soy sauce and chicken stock. Simmer for 2 minutes, taste and check the seasoning, add the noodles, and combine thoroughly.

Divide between 2 bowls and serve sprinkled with the scallions.

for the *dashi*

4-inch piece of *konbu* (kelp)
    seaweed
handful of dried bonito flakes
    (*katsuo bushi*, see page 11)

for the dipping sauce

3 tablespoons soy sauce
1 tablespoon lemon juice or *mirin*

3½ ounces egg noodles
7 ounces beef (boneless top loin
    steak), thinly sliced
4 shiitake mushrooms
3½ ounces enoki mushrooms
2 carrots, peeled and thinly sliced
2 scallions, cut on the
    diagonal
handful of baby spinach
2 ounces *kamaboko-aka* (see
    page 11), sliced 5mm thick
3½ ounces firm tofu, cubed

heating element to use at the table

poached beef and noodles with mushrooms and tofu

Lightly brush the *konbu* with a damp cloth. Place in a saucepan and cover with 1 quart water. Bring to a boil. Remove from the heat, take out the *konbu*, and discard. Add the bonito flakes, return to the heat, and bring almost to a boil. Remove from the heat and wait for the bonito to sink to the bottom. Strain. If you leave the bonito in for too long, it adds a bitter note. You have now made primary *dashi*.

Bring the *dashi* almost to a boil and transfer to the table over your heating element.

In a small serving bowl, combine the soy sauce and lemon juice to make the dipping sauce. Cook the noodles according to the instructions on the package, drain, refresh under cold water, and transfer to a plate.

Arrange the meat, vegetables, *kamaboko-aka*, and tofu in lines with the noodles at one end.

Each person then "cooks" the various ingredients in the broth. The beef takes very little time, say a minute, while some of the vegetables take 2 or 3 minutes. Dip in the sauce and eat. When you have finished poaching all the ingredients, pile the noodles into your bowl, ladle over the enriched *dashi*, and eat as a soup.

If you are in a hurry, you can skip making the primary dashi *and use an instant version,* dashi no moto *(see page 11). A pan set over a tea light or two makes a good heating element.*

4 wooden skewers, soaked for
    1 hour beforehand

for the marinade
1 lemongrass stalk, outer leaves
    removed, finely chopped
2 garlic cloves, peeled and minced
1 teaspoon sesame seed, briefly
    toasted in a hot, dry skillet
1 chile, finely sliced
pinch of sugar
1 tablespoon soy sauce
2 teaspoons fish sauce (nam pla)

4½ ounces beef (boneless top loin
    steak), trimmed and cut into
    strips
½-inch piece of fresh ginger, peeled
    and grated
2 teaspoons oyster sauce
1 tablespoon mirin (see page 11)
2 teaspoons tahini paste
3½ ounces fresh egg noodles
¼ cup roughly chopped roasted
    peanuts
handful of cilantro, leaves picked
handful of mint, leaves picked
6 Thai basil leaves
4 Bibb lettuce leaves, roughly
    chopped
2 scallions, finely sliced

marinated beef skewers and egg noodles

In a medium bowl, combine the marinade ingredients, taste, and season with salt and black pepper if required. Add the beef, mixing to coat well. (This part is important—if you simply toss the beef, it will not take on as much flavor from the marinade.) Cover and set aside for an hour, or better still, place in the fridge overnight.

Thread the beef strips onto the soaked skewers, concertina style. Preheat the broiler to high. Place the skewers on a tray under the broiler and cook for 2 minutes each side; longer if you prefer your meat well done.

In a small bowl, combine the ginger, oyster sauce, mirin, and tahini paste to make a thick dressing. Cook the noodles according to the instructions on the package, drain, then return them to the pan and add the dressing and peanuts. Lightly toss to mix. You may need a little hot water if the paste is too thick.

Divide the noodles between 2 plates and top with the broiled meat skewers. Serve sprinkled with the cilantro, mint, basil, and lettuce leaves, and scallions.

desserts

14 **wild berry so___t** £2.75
2 scoops of ___ berry sorbet garnished with
fresh blueb___s and a sprig of mint

15 **lime ar___em ginger tart** £4.25
swee___stry base filled with lime and stem
___ger ___lard. served with crème fraiche and
___vi___lime zest

16 **___ut reika** £2.95
3 ___ps of dairy coconut ice cream topped
___resh passion fruit sauce and toasted
___flakes

17 **white ___ocolate and ginger cheesecake** £4.25
creamy ___ite chocolate and glacé stem ginger
cheese___ on a crunchy ginger biscuit base
topped ___ white chocolate shavings

18 **chocolat___dge cake** £4.25
rich chocol___ udge cake with a wasabi and
white choco___ fudge filling. served with dairy
vanilla ice c___

19 **natural fruit l___llies** £1.50
ask your serve___ oday's choice

one-pot

Some dishes are more than soup, but not quite a stir-fry. A little like a casserole or stew. Something hearty and warming. A bit of stir-frying may be involved, but the finished dish tends to be in a pot, hence one-pot. Or one-wok as, confusingly, sometimes a wok is the best pot.

The dishes in this chapter tend to be of a robust nature. Lots of ingredients, lots of flavors, lots of attitude. Which is why we like them. Yet with so many items it is important to retain control.

One-pot cooking suits most of us. Minimal washing up for a start. But there is also a welcome simplicity. No sense of madness with multiple hot-plates on the go. We like a sense of calm and order in our kitchens. It is important.

One-pot cooking is very focused. It allows you to proceed in a very ordered way. Which is a good thing in a kitchen. Why complicate things when they don't need to be?

These dishes are meant to be shared at the table rather than plated up, as we do in the restaurants (or indeed as we suggest in many of the other chapters). That way you get to eat as you want. And a bit more doesn't seem like a dramatic move. Or a bit less for that matter.

These dishes are also a bit slower than elsewhere in this book. There is more of an opportunity for ingredients to get to know each other. Whereas a stir-fry comes hot off the pan, these dishes are far more mellow. Laid-back, even.

stir-fried greens with plum sauce

serves 2

3½ ounces medium egg noodles

1 tablespoon vegetable oil

2 cups small broccoli florets

1 small onion, peeled and cut
vertically into eighths

1¼-inch piece of fresh ginger,
peeled and finely grated

1 garlic clove, peeled and minced

1 head of bok choy, leaves
separated

2 tablespoons plum sauce

1 red chile, seeded and finely
sliced

1 tablespoon soy sauce

⅓ cup chicken stock (see page 13)

2 teaspoons cornstarch, dissolved
in 2 tablespoons of the
chicken stock

salt and white pepper

Cook the noodles according to the instructions on the package, drain, and refresh under cold water.

In a hot wok, heat the vegetable oil and stir-fry the broccoli and onion for 2 minutes. Add the ginger, garlic, and bok choy, and toss well for 2 to 3 minutes. Add the plum sauce, chile, and soy sauce and cook for another 2 minutes.

Add the chicken stock and dissolved cornstarch and stir until everything thickens, about 30 seconds, then add the noodles. Toss to ensure that everything is well coated, taste and adjust the seasoning, and serve.

stir-fried vegetables with cellophane noodles

serves 2

4½ ounces cellophane noodles

1 tablespoon vegetable oil

1 green chile, finely sliced

1 garlic clove, peeled and minced

1 teaspoon brown sugar

4 shiitake mushrooms, sliced

1 small carrot, peeled and julienned

1 red onion, peeled and cut into
thin half-moon slices

½ head of Chinese cabbage, sliced

3 teaspoons soy sauce

juice of ½ lemon

2 teaspoons toasted sesame oil

1 tablespoon finely sliced scallion

In a medium bowl, soak the noodles in warm water until soft, about 5 minutes. Drain, refresh under cold water, and roughly chop.

Add the vegetable oil to a hot wok over medium heat and stir-fry the chile and garlic for 30 seconds. Add the sugar and cook for another 30 seconds. Turn the heat up and add the mushrooms, carrot, red onion, and Chinese cabbage. Stir-fry until the vegetables just start to color, about 3 to 4 minutes.

Add the noodles and soy sauce and stir-fry until the vegetables are just cooked, about another 3 minutes. Remove from the heat and add the lemon juice and sesame oil, tossing thoroughly to disperse evenly.

Serve sprinkled with the scallion.

braised summer vegetables with tofu

2 tablespoons vegetable oil

5 ounces firm tofu, cut into 1¼-inch
    x 1¼-inch x ½-inch slices

1 tablespoon red curry paste
    (see page 16)

1⅔ cups chicken or vegetable stock
    (see page 13)

1 tablespoon soy sauce

2 teaspoons sake

½ cup soy milk

2 yellow zucchini, cut into
    ¼-inch disks

heaping ½ cup frozen peas, defrosted

1 tablespoon finely sliced button
    mushrooms

2 teaspoons fish sauce (*nam pla*)

2 ounces wide rice noodles

salt and white pepper

2 scallions, green parts
    included, thinly sliced

In a hot wok, heat the oil and sauté the tofu until well colored, about 2 minutes each side. Remove and set aside.

Pour off the oil and add the curry paste. Cook over medium heat until it starts to lose its raw aroma, about 1 minute. Add the stock, soy sauce, sake, and soy milk, bring to a boil and add the vegetables and fish sauce. Cook over medium heat until the vegetables are just tender but with some bite, about 4 minutes.

Cook the noodles according to the instructions on the package, drain, and refresh under cold water.

Divide between 2 bowls. Return the tofu to the wok, check the seasoning, and pour over the noodles. Serve scattered with the scallions.

teriyaki tofu steaks with glazed green vegetables

3½ ounces cellophane noodles

2 tablespoons soy sauce

2 tablespoons *mirin* (see page 11)

2 tablespoons sake

1 teaspoon sugar

7 ounces tofu, cut into steaks

2 shiitake mushrooms, sliced

1 garlic clove, peeled and finely
    chopped

1 heaping cup roughly chopped
    broccoli florets

1 leek, sliced

3½ ounces bok choy, roughly
    chopped

½ fennel bulb, thinly sliced

2 teaspoons cornstarch

1 teaspoon sesame seed, briefly
    toasted in a hot, dry skillet

Cook the noodles according to the instructions on the package, drain, and refresh under cold water. In a wok, heat the soy sauce, *mirin*, sake, and sugar until the sugar dissolves. Add the tofu and mushrooms and simmer for 15 minutes.

Stir in the garlic and vegetables and simmer until just soft, about 10 minutes. Dissolve the cornstarch in 1 tablespoon water and add to the wok to thicken. Simmer for 2 minutes. Stir in the noodles and serve sprinkled with the sesame seed.

mushroom egg noodles

serves 2

3½ ounces medium egg noodles

3 tablespoons vegetable oil

3 garlic cloves, peeled and minced

1¼-inch piece of fresh ginger,
    peeled and grated

7 ounces mixed mushrooms,
    such as enoki, oyster, shiitake,
    button, or portobello, trimmed
    and large ones torn in half

2 tablespoons canned, drained
    bamboo shoots

4½ ounces (about a scant ⅔ cup)
    canned water chestnuts,
    rinsed, drained, and halved
    if large

2 scallions, cut into 1¼-inch lengths

½ red bell pepper, seeded and
    thinly sliced

2 tablespoons *tori kara age* sauce
    (see page 21)

salt and white pepper

2 handfuls of bean sprouts

Cook the noodles according to the instructions on the package, drain, and refresh under cold water.

In a hot wok, heat 2 tablespoons of the oil over high heat and stir-fry the garlic and ginger for 30 seconds, then add all the mushrooms, bamboo shoots, water chestnuts, scallions, and red bell pepper. Stir-fry until the vegetables are just cooked, about 2 to 3 minutes, remove, and set aside.

Wipe the wok clean and reheat. Add the remaining oil and stir-fry the noodles for 1 minute. Add the *tori kara age* sauce and continue cooking for 2 minutes. Return the mushroom mix and toss through to ensure that everything is heated through. Check the seasoning, top with the bean sprouts, and serve.

wide noodle hot-pot with seven vegetables

serves 2

2 small heads of bok choy,
    quartered lengthways
1 cup small broccoli florets
2 ounces wide rice noodles
⅔ cup chicken stock (see page 13)
2 tablespoons *mirin* (see page 11)
3 tablespoons soy sauce
2 teaspoons sugar
1 garlic clove, peeled and mashed
¾-inch piece of fresh ginger, peeled
    and grated
1 red chile, chopped
handful of finely shredded Chinese
    cabbage
handful of snow peas
2 carrots, peeled and thinly sliced
1 small zucchini, thinly sliced
4 shiitake mushrooms, thinly sliced
handful of cilantro leaves

In a saucepan, blanch the bok choy and broccoli in boiling salted water until just tender. Drain and refresh under cold water.

Cook the noodles according to the instructions on the package, drain, and refresh under cold water.

In a heavy, lidded saucepan, place the stock, *mirin,* soy sauce, sugar, garlic, ginger, and chile, cover, and bring to a boil. Add the Chinese cabbage, snow peas, carrots, zucchini, and mushrooms and cook until softened but still crunchy, about 4 minutes. Add the blanched vegetables and noodles, check the seasoning, and simmer over gentle heat for 2 minutes. Let rest for 2 minutes, stir in the cilantro, and serve.

eggplant hot-pot

serves 2

1 medium eggplant, cut into
    ¾-inch dice
salt and white pepper
4 tablespoons vegetable oil
2 tablespoons finely chopped
    shallots
2 red chiles, chopped
3 garlic cloves, peeled and chopped
1¼-inch piece of fresh ginger,
    peeled and finely chopped
3 lemongrass stalks, outer leaves
    removed, finely chopped
3 tablespoons *mirin* (see page 11)
2 cups vegetable or chicken stock
    (see page 13)
3½ ounces *udon* noodles
4 handfuls of baby spinach
bunch of cilantro, leaves picked

Sprinkle the eggplant with salt, place in a colander, and set aside for 30 minutes. Rinse thoroughly in plenty of cold water and pat dry.

In a hot wok, heat 2 tablespoons of the oil and stir-fry the eggplant until the pieces are golden brown, about 5 to 6 minutes. (You may need to do this in batches; if the wok is overcrowded everything will stew.) Remove and drain on paper towels.

Reheat the wok, then add the remaining oil and stir-fry the shallots, chile, garlic, ginger, and lemongrass for 3 minutes. Add the eggplant, *mirin*, and stock and season with salt and pepper.

Reduce the heat and simmer for 10 minutes. Add the noodles and spinach and cook until the noodles are just tender and the liquid has thickened, about 6 to 8 minutes. Stir in the cilantro, check the seasoning, and serve.

hot and sour shrimp noodles

7 ounces raw, peeled shrimp,
    deveined
1 tablespoon lemon juice
1 teaspoon peeled and minced
    fresh ginger
4 garlic cloves, peeled and mashed
¾ cup chicken stock (see
    page 13)
2 tablespoons *mirin* (see page 11)
2 tablespoons soy sauce
2 tablespoons chili *ramen* sauce
    (see page 18)
2 teaspoons cornstarch
3½ ounces *udon* noodles
2 tablespoons vegetable oil
1 small onion, peeled and
    thinly sliced
1 teaspoon hot chili paste
generous handful of baby spinach
generous handful of bean sprouts

In a medium bowl, toss the shrimp with the lemon juice, ginger, and half the garlic. Cover and set aside for 30 minutes. Combine the chicken stock, *mirin*, soy sauce, chili *ramen* sauce, and cornstarch and set aside.

Cook the noodles according to the instructions on the package, drain, and rinse under cold water.

Heat a wok over high heat, add 1 tablespoon of the oil, and stir-fry the shrimp until cooked, about 2 minutes. Remove and set aside.

Wipe the wok clean and reheat over medium heat, adding the remaining oil. Stir-fry the onion and remaining garlic with the chili paste until softened and just coloring, about 2 minutes. Add the chicken stock mixture and simmer for 3 minutes, stirring constantly.

When the sauce has thickened, add the shrimp, noodles, and spinach. Mix gently for 1 minute to ensure that everything is heated through, top with the bean sprouts, and serve.

3½ ounces *udon* noodles

2 tablespoons soy sauce

1 tablespoon *mirin* (see page 11)

2 teaspoons fish sauce (*nam pla*)

1¼-inch piece of fresh ginger,
  peeled and grated

12 small clams, rinsed and drained

3½ ounces shiitake mushrooms, cut
  into ½-inch strips

5 ounces sea bass (branzini) fillets,
  cut into ½-inch pieces

8 raw shrimp, peeled but tails
  on and deveined

1 sheet of dried *nori* seaweed,
  cut into ½-inch strips

3½ ounces tofu, cubed

1 small head Bibb lettuce, shredded

salt and white pepper

½ roll (3½ ounces) *kamaboko-aka*
  (see page 11), in ½-inch slices

seafood stew

Cook the noodles according to the instructions on the package, drain, and refresh under cold water.

Heat a heavy, lidded saucepan over medium heat. Combine the soy sauce, *mirin,* fish sauce, and ginger with ¾ cup water and add to the pan. When the mixture is boiling, add the clams. Put the lid on and steam until the shells start to open, about 2 minutes. Lift out the clams.

Add the mushrooms and sea bass, cover, and cook for 2 minutes. Add the shrimp and cook for another 2 minutes with the lid on. Return the clams along with the seaweed, noodles, tofu, and lettuce. Season with salt and pepper, cover, and allow to sit for another 3 minutes. Discard any clams that remain closed.

Serve with the slices of *kamaboko-aka* scattered over.

serves 2

3½ ounces rice noodles

2 tablespoons vegetable oil

2 large eggs, lightly beaten and
  seasoned

7 ounces raw, peeled shrimp,
  deveined

2 garlic cloves, peeled and finely
  chopped

1 chile, seeded and finely chopped

1 tablespoon fish sauce (*nam pla*)

1 tablespoon soy sauce

½ teaspoon brown sugar

handful of bean sprouts

2 teaspoons dried shrimp, rinsed

2 scallions, finely sliced

salt and white pepper

1 tablespoon chopped roasted
  peanuts

small bunch of cilantro,
  leaves picked

1 lime, halved

sweet and sour shrimp noodles

Cook the noodles according to the instructions on the package, drain, and refresh under cold water.

In a hot wok, heat 1 tablespoon of the oil, then add the egg, swirl around so that it thinly coats the bottom of the wok, and cook until set, about 1 minute. Remove, let cool, then roll up and thinly slice.

Heat the remaining oil in the hot wok and stir-fry the shrimp, garlic, and chile until cooked, a scant 2 minutes. Add the fish sauce, soy sauce, sugar, and noodles and stir-fry for 1 minute. Add the bean sprouts, dried shrimp, scallions and reserved egg strips, toss well, and check the seasoning. Serve topped with the peanuts and cilantro and the lime halves.

spiced mussels with wide rice noodles

5 ounces wide rice noodles

1 tablespoon vegetable oil

1 onion, peeled and thinly sliced

1¼-inch piece of fresh ginger, peeled and grated

3 garlic cloves, peeled and minced

1 green chile, seeded and finely chopped

½ teaspoon turmeric

2 star anise

large bunch of cilantro, leaves picked, stems finely chopped

¾ cup coconut milk

1 pound mussels, scrubbed and debearded

Cook the noodles according to the instructions on the package, drain, and refresh under cold water.

In a hot wok, heat the vegetable oil and stir-fry the onion until softened and just catching color, about 2 minutes. Add the ginger, garlic, chile, and turmeric and cook for another minute, taking care not to let the mixture catch on the bottom.

Add the star anise and cilantro stems and continue cooking for 30 seconds before adding the coconut milk. Bring to a boil, reduce the heat, and let simmer so that everything thickens, about 1 minute.

Add the mussels, turn up the heat, and cover. Cook until the mussels start to open, about 5 minutes. Remove the cover, stir in the noodles, and toss to ensure that everything is heated through and well coated. Discard any mussels that remain closed.

Serve scattered with the reserved cilantro leaves.

serves 2

3½ ounces rice noodles

1 tablespoon vegetable oil

2 garlic cloves, peeled and minced

1 red onion, peeled and thinly
    sliced

1 small head of broccoli, broken
    into florets

4 asparagus spears, trimmed

5 ounces prepared squid, scored
    and cut into 1¼-inch pieces

1 tablespoon soy sauce

1 teaspoon cornstarch

¾ cup chicken stock (see page 13)

salt and white pepper

1 red chile, finely sliced

squid, broccoli, and asparagus

Cook the noodles according to the instructions on the package, drain, and refresh under cold water. Toss with 1 teaspoon of the oil.

In a hot wok, heat the remaining oil and stir-fry the garlic, red onion, broccoli, asparagus, and squid until they just start to color, about 4 to 5 minutes. Combine the soy sauce and cornstarch. Add the chicken stock and the cornstarch mixture and simmer for 3 minutes. Add the noodles to the pan. Stir to ensure everything is well coated, and check the seasoning.

Serve with a scattering of the sliced chile.

serves 2

3½ ounces rice noodles

2 tablespoons vegetable oil

2 large eggs, beaten and seasoned

12 raw, peeled shrimp, deveined

salt and white pepper

6 shiitake mushrooms, sliced

6 scallions, cut into 1¼-inch lengths

2 garlic cloves, peeled and minced

3 tablespoons hoisin sauce

3 tablespoons chicken stock
    (see page 13)

1⅔ cups spinach leaves

2 handfuls of bean sprouts

shrimp, mushroom and spinach noodles

Cook the noodles according to the instructions on the package, drain, and refresh under cold water.

In a hot wok, heat 1 tablespoon of the oil, then add the egg, swirl around so that it thinly coats the bottom of the wok, and cook until set, about 1 minute. Remove, let cool, then roll up and thinly slice.

Clean the wok and reheat. Heat the remaining oil, season the shrimp and stir-fry for 2 to 3 minutes. Add the mushrooms and scallions and stir-fry for 1 minute. Add the garlic and, 10 seconds later, the hoisin sauce and stock. Bring to a boil, cook for 1 minute, and then add the spinach. Cook until the shrimp are done, another 2 minutes.

Fold in the noodles and shredded egg, check the seasoning, and serve topped with the bean sprouts.

spiced shrimp with egg noodles and water chestnuts

serves 2

3½ ounces medium egg noodles
1 tablespoon vegetable oil
2 garlic cloves, peeled and roughly chopped
1¼-inch piece of fresh ginger, peeled and grated
1 chile, seeded and finely sliced
7 ounces raw, peeled shrimp, deveined
bunch of cilantro, leaves picked, stems finely chopped
salt and white pepper
1 tablespoon oyster sauce
1 tablespoon *mirin* (see page 11)
1 tablespoon fish sauce (*nam pla*)
10 canned water chestnuts, rinsed and drained
1 teaspoon toasted sesame oil

Cook the noodles according to the instructions on the package, drain, and refresh under cold water. Toss with 1 teaspoon of the vegetable oil.

In a hot wok, heat the remaining vegetable oil and add the garlic. Sauté for 30 seconds, then remove the garlic from the pan and reserve. Add the ginger, chile, shrimp, and the cilantro stems, season with salt and pepper, and stir-fry until the shrimp are cooked, about 2 to 3 minutes.

Add the cooked noodles along with the oyster sauce, *mirin,* fish sauce, water chestnuts, and sesame oil and simmer for 1 minute, stirring to combine and coat. Remove from the heat, stir in the reserved cilantro leaves, and check the seasoning. Serve scattered with the reserved garlic.

thai-style seafood noodle curry

serves 2

3½ ounces rice vermicelli
1 tablespoon vegetable oil
3 ounces prepared squid, cut into 1¼-inch pieces
6 raw, unpeeled shrimp, deveined
salt and white pepper
¾ cup coconut milk
2 teaspoons dried shrimp, well rinsed
2 teaspoons fish sauce (*nam pla*)
1 tablespoon soy sauce
1 chile, finely sliced
1¼-inch piece of fresh ginger, peeled and grated
12 mussels, scrubbed and debearded
bunch of cilantro, leaves picked

Cook the vermicelli according to the instructions on the package, drain, and refresh under cold water.

In a hot wok, heat the oil. Season the squid and shrimp with salt and stir-fry until cooked, about 2 to 3 minutes. Remove and set aside.

Add the coconut milk, dried shrimp, fish sauce, soy sauce, chile, and ginger to the wok and bring to a boil. Add the mussels and as soon as they start to open add the noodles. Stir well to ensure that everything is well combined, then add the reserved seafood. Discard any mussels that remain closed. Toss gently, check the seasoning, and serve scattered with the cilantro leaves.

serves 2

1 tablespoon vegetable oil

2 teaspoons finely chopped
    shallots

2 teaspoons red curry paste (see
    page 16)

½ cup coconut milk

1 teaspoon dark brown sugar

2 teaspoons fish sauce (*nam pla*)

finely grated zest and juice of
    1 lime, plus 1 lime, cut into
    wedges

2 skinless salmon fillets, about
    3½ ounces each

small handful of Thai basil leaves

small handful of mint leaves

3½ ounces wide rice noodles

salmon curry with rice noodles

Heat a sauté pan large enough to accommodate the salmon over medium heat. Add the oil and shallots and cook until soft without coloring, about 2 minutes.

Add the red curry paste and continue to cook for 2 minutes, stirring constantly. Add the coconut milk, sugar, fish sauce, and the lime zest and juice. Bring to a boil, then reduce to a gentle simmer for 5 minutes. Taste and adjust the seasoning.

Ease the salmon fillets into the sauce and gently poach until the fish is cooked, about 8 to 10 minutes (depending on the thickness). Add the basil and mint.

Cook the noodles according to the instructions on the package and drain immediately. Gently stir the noodles into the pot. Serve with the lime wedges on the side.

marinated salmon, bok choy, and black bean sauce

serves 2

for the marinade

2 teaspoons soy sauce

pinch of sugar

2 teaspoons *mirin* (see page 11)

2 teaspoons vegetable oil

salt and white pepper

7 ounces salmon fillets, cutlets, or
    tail end, cut into 2 pieces

3½ ounces *ramen* noodles

1 tablespoon vegetable oil

1 onion, peeled and finely sliced

1 small red bell pepper, seeded and
    thinly sliced

1¼-inch piece of fresh ginger,
    peeled and grated

2 garlic cloves, peeled and minced

1 tablespoon black bean sauce

1 red chile, seeded and finely
    sliced

1 cup chicken stock (see page 13)

2 teaspoons cornstarch,
    dissolved in 2 tablespoons
    cold water

2 heads of bok choy, sliced very
    thinly lengthwise

In a medium bowl, combine the marinade ingredients and season with salt and pepper. Add the salmon and turn to coat thoroughly. Cover and set aside for at least 1 hour; overnight in the fridge is even better.

Cook the noodles according to the instructions on the package, drain, and refresh under cold water.

Preheat the broiler or grill to high. Remove the salmon pieces (reserve the marinade) and cook the salmon until cooked through, turning once, about 5 minutes.

In a hot wok, heat the vegetable oil, and stir-fry the onion, red bell pepper, ginger, and garlic for 1 minute. Add the black bean sauce, chile, chicken stock, reserved marinade, and dissolved cornstarch and simmer for 2 minutes. Stir in the noodles and bok choy until the bok choy has wilted, about another minute.

Top with the salmon and serve.

marinated monkfish with broccoli and oyster sauce

1¼-inch piece of fresh ginger,
    peeled and grated
3 garlic cloves, peeled and grated
1 tablespoon *mirin* (see page 11)
2 teaspoons fish sauce (*nam pla*)

7 ounces monkfish fillet, cut into
    ½-inch disks
3½ ounces thin egg noodles
3 cups broccoli florets
salt and white pepper
1 tablespoon vegetable oil
2 tablespoons oyster sauce
4 scallions, finely sliced
1 red chile, finely sliced
2 teaspoons sesame seed, briefly
    toasted in a hot, dry skillet
2 teaspoons toasted sesame oil

In a medium bowl, combine the marinade ingredients. Add the monkfish to the marinade, and turn to coat thoroughly. Cover and set aside for a few hours in the fridge; overnight is even better.

Cook the noodles according to the instructions on the package, drain, and refresh under cold water. In a saucepan, blanch the broccoli in boiling salted water until just tender, drain, and refresh under cold water.

In a hot wok, heat the vegetable oil and stir-fry the monkfish for 2 minutes. Add the broccoli and stir-fry for 1 minute. Add the oyster sauce, check the seasoning, then stir in the drained noodles.

Serve scattered with the scallions, chile, sesame seed and a drizzle of sesame oil.

serves 2

stir-fried sea bass with spinach and scallions

3½ ounces *somen* noodles
7 ounces spinach
1¼-inch piece of fresh ginger,
    peeled and grated
1 tablespoon soy sauce
2 garlic cloves, peeled and
    thinly sliced
juice of 1 lemon
1 teaspoon fish sauce (*nam pla*)
1 teaspoon rice vinegar
1 tablespoon vegetable oil
4 scallions, cut into 1¼-inch lengths
2 teaspoons cornstarch, seasoned
    with salt and white pepper
7 ounces sea bass (branzini) fillets
    (skin on), cut into bite-size
    pieces
2 teaspoons toasted sesame oil
1 teaspoon sesame seed, briefly
    toasted in a hot, dry skillet

Cook the noodles according to the instructions on the package, drain, and refresh under cold water.

In a saucepan, blanch the spinach in boiling salted water until just wilted, about 30 seconds. Drain, refresh under cold water, and squeeze gently. Fluff up the spinach and set aside.

In a small bowl, combine the ginger, soy sauce, garlic, lemon juice, fish sauce, and rice vinegar. In a hot wok, heat the vegetable oil and stir-fry the scallions until they just start to color, about 1 minute.

Dust the sea bass with the seasoned cornstarch. Add to the pan and stir-fry for until the fish is almost cooked, about 2 to 3 minutes. Add the spinach, noodles, and the ginger mixture and cook until everything is amalgamated and bubbling. Remove from the heat, pour over the sesame oil, and serve scattered with the sesame seed.

peppered mackerel with ramen noodles

serves 2

½ teaspoon szechwan peppercorns
½ teaspoon black peppercorns
7 ounces *ramen* noodles
1 tablespoon vegetable oil
2 small red onions, peeled and cut
    vertically into eighths
2 teaspoons oyster sauce
2 teaspoons hoisin sauce
1 teaspoon cornstarch, dissolved in
    2 tablespoons water
juice of 1 lime
5 ounces skinless mackerel fillet,
    cut into bite-size pieces
handful of bean sprouts

Heat a dry skillet and toast the peppercorns together until they release their aromas. Transfer to a pestle and mortar and crush.

Cook the noodles according to the instructions on the package, drain, and refresh under cold water.

In a hot wok, heat the vegetable oil and stir-fry the crushed peppercorns and red onions until the onions start to color, about 4 minutes.

Combine the oyster sauce, hoisin sauce, cornstarch, and lime juice. Add this mixture and the mackerel to the wok and stir-fry until the fish is cooked, about 2 minutes. Add the noodles and toss well to ensure everything is well coated.

Serve topped with the bean sprouts.

shrimp and chicken noodles

serves 2

3½ ounces medium egg noodles
1 tablespoon vegetable oil
1 tablespoon shallots, peeled and
    cut into half-moon slices
1¼-inch piece of fresh ginger,
    peeled and finely chopped
2 garlic cloves, peeled and chopped
3½ ounces ground chicken
3½ ounces raw, peeled shrimp,
    deveined
handful of finely sliced Chinese
    cabbage
⅔ cup chopped canned water
    chestnuts
1 large egg, lightly beaten and
    seasoned
1 tablespoon curry powder
2 tablespoons soy sauce
1 tablespoon *mirin* (see page 11)
1 teaspoon sugar
handful of bean sprouts
2 tablespoons oyster sauce
2 teaspoons toasted sesame oil
2 scallions, finely sliced

Cook the noodles according to the instructions on the package, drain, and refresh under cold water.

In a hot wok, heat the vegetable oil and stir-fry the shallots, ginger, and garlic for 1 minute. Add the chicken, shrimp, Chinese cabbage, and water chestnuts and stir-fry for 2 minutes. Add the egg, stirring it into the other ingredients for about 30 seconds.

Add the curry powder, soy sauce, *mirin,* and sugar along with the noodles and bean sprouts and toss everything to heat through for 1 minute. Remove from the heat and stir in the oyster sauce and sesame oil.

Serve topped with the scallions.

chicken curry noodles

serves 2

3 tablespoons vegetable oil

5 ounces boneless, skinless chicken breast, diced

1 zucchini, diced

½ small eggplant, diced

2 scallions, cut into ½-inch pieces

1 garlic clove, peeled and finely chopped

1¼-inch piece of fresh ginger, peeled and finely chopped

1 tablespoon green curry paste (see page 18)

1 cup chicken stock (see page 13)

¾ cup coconut milk

1 tablespoon fish sauce (*nam pla*)

3½ ounces medium egg noodles

juice of 1 lime

salt and white pepper

2 tablespoons roughly chopped cilantro

2 tablespoons unsalted peanuts

In a hot wok, heat 1 tablespoon of the vegetable oil over medium heat and stir-fry the chicken until golden brown, about 3 to 4 minutes. Remove and set aside.

Add the remaining oil to the wok and stir-fry the zucchini and eggplant until golden brown, about 4 minutes. The eggplant tends to soak up the oil at first and then release it.

Add the scallions, stir-fry for 1 minute, and then add the garlic and ginger. Cook for 1 minute and then stir in the curry paste.

Pour in the chicken stock, coconut milk, and fish sauce, bring to a boil and simmer for 10 minutes. Add the noodles and reserved chicken and cook until the noodles are tender, about 4 minutes. Add the lime juice and check the seasoning.

Serve sprinkled with the cilantro and peanuts.

stir-fried shrimp and pork with crispy noodles

serves 2

3½ ounces raw, peeled shrimp, deveined

2 ounces rice vermicelli

vegetable oil, for frying

2 tablespoons finely chopped shallots

3 garlic cloves, peeled and finely sliced

pinch of crushed red pepper (or to taste)

7 ounces ground pork

large handful of bean sprouts

½ teaspoon light brown sugar

1 tablespoon fish sauce (*nam pla*)

1 tablespoon *mirin* (see page 11)

small handful of cilantro leaves

juice of 1 lime

Butterfly the shrimp: Cut each one lengthwise almost right the way through, and open out the 2 halves.

Put the vermicelli into a small plastic food bag and break into short lengths. Heat 1¼ inches of oil in a wok to 350°F (drop in a piece of vermicelli: it will puff up if the oil is hot enough). Cook the noodles in batches: they puff up immediately, so you need to extract them quickly. Drain on paper towel as they are cooked.

In a hot wok, heat 1 tablespoon oil and stir-fry the shallots for 1 minute. Add the garlic, crushed red pepper, and pork and continue stir-frying until the pork is almost cooked, another 2 minutes. Add the shrimp, bean sprouts, sugar, fish sauce, and *mirin* and continue stir-frying until the shrimp are cooked, about another 2 to 3 minutes. Toss the cilantro through.

Serve the pork and shrimp mixture on top of the noodles with the lime juice squeezed over.

pork, shrimp, rice and noodle hot-pot

serves 2

3½ ounces pork tenderloin, thinly sliced

2 garlic cloves, peeled and crushed

2 tablespoons soy sauce

⅓ cup plus 1 tablespoon basmati rice

4 small dried shiitake mushrooms

1 tablespoon vegetable oil

3½ ounces raw, peeled shrimp, deveined

2 cups chicken stock (see page 13)

1 tablespoon fish sauce (*nam pla*)

3 ounces medium egg noodles, broken into 1½-inch lengths

2 bok choy, quartered lengthwise

salt and white pepper

1 lime, cut into wedges

In a medium bowl, combine the pork, garlic, and soy sauce and set aside.

Rinse the rice in plenty of cold water and let stand, covered by a good few inches of cold water for 30 minutes, or an hour if possible.

Place the mushrooms in a small heatproof bowl, pour boiling water over them, and set aside until soft, about 20 minutes. Slice the mushrooms, reserving the liquid.

In a hot wok, heat the oil and sauté the pork, garlic, and soy sauce for 1 minute. Stir in the shrimp, mushrooms, and mushroom liquid, and sauté for another minute. Add the stock and fish sauce. Bring to a boil, add the rice, and cook gently for about 5 minutes, then add the noodles and bok choy and continue cooking until both the rice and noodles are cooked, about another 4 minutes.

Check the seasoning and serve with the lime wedges.

If you don't soak the rice it takes much longer to cook, which makes adding the noodles at the right time difficult.

stir-fried pork noodles

serves 2

for the marinade

1 garlic clove, peeled and chopped
    then crushed with a little salt
1¼-inch piece of fresh ginger,
    peeled and grated
1 tablespoon soy sauce

3½ ounces pork tenderloin, cut into
    thin strips
5 ounces rice vermicelli
1 tablespoon dried shrimp, well
    rinsed
handful of green beans, trimmed
1 tablespoon vegetable oil
¾ cup finely sliced button mushrooms
2 handfuls of spinach
soy sauce
2 scallions, finely sliced

In a medium bowl, combine the marinade ingredients. Add the pork, toss well, cover, and set aside for 1 hour or so; overnight in the fridge is even better.

Cook the vermicelli according to the instructions on the package, drain, and refesh under cold water.

In a small heatproof bowl, soak the shrimp in boiling water for 10 minutes, then strain, reserving the liquid. In a saucepan, cook the beans in salted water until just tender but with some bite, drain, and refresh under cold water.

In a hot wok, heat the oil and stir-fry the mushrooms, pork, and its marinade for 3 minutes. Add the beans and spinach and stir-fry until wilted, about 1 minute. Add the vermicelli and reserved shrimp liquid and season with soy sauce to taste.

Serve with the reserved shrimp and scallions scattered over the top.

marinated pork and cellophane noodles

serves 2

for the marinade

1 tablespoon soy sauce
1 tablespoon *mirin* (see page 11)
1 teaspoon chili oil
2 teaspoons peeled and grated
    fresh ginger
2 garlic cloves, peeled and crushed

7 ounces pork tenderloin,
    trimmed and sliced
3 ounces cellophane noodles
2 tablespoons vegetable oil
4 scallions, cut into 1¼-inch
    pieces
2 heads of bok choy, roughly
    chopped
small bunch of cilantro, roughly
    chopped
1 teaspoon cornstarch
⅓ cup chicken stock (see page 13)
salt and white pepper

In a medium bowl, combine the marinade ingredients, add the pork, and stir to combine well. Cover and leave for 30 minutes; overnight in the fridge is even better. Drain and reserve the excess marinade.

Cook the noodles according to the instructions on the package, drain, and refresh under cold water.

In a wok, heat the oil, then add the pork and stir-fry to seal, 2 minutes. Add the scallions, bok choy, and cilantro and stir-fry for another minute.

Mix the cornstarch with a little of the chicken stock. Add this to the wok with the remaining stock and the reserved marinade, and cook for 1 minute. Add the noodles and continue cooking until everything is thick and syrupy. Taste and adjust the seasoning before serving.

marinated pork and tofu with rice noodles

for the marinade

1¼-inch piece of fresh ginger,
    peeled and grated
2 garlic cloves, peeled and minced
    or grated
1 tablespoon soy sauce

3½ ounces pork tenderloin,
    trimmed and cut into strips
salt and white pepper
5 ounces rice noodles
2 tablespoons vegetable oil
2½ ounces tofu, in one piece
¼ cup unsalted peanuts
1 garlic clove, peeled and crushed
1 small red onion, peeled and
    thinly sliced
1 green chile, seeded and
    thinly sliced
1 cup bean sprouts
2½ ounces Chinese flowering
    chives (see page 11),
    finely sliced
1 tablespoon dark soy sauce
cilantro leaves

In a medium bowl, combine the marinade ingredients. Add the pork, mix thoroughly, and season. Cover and set aside for 1 hour; overnight in the fridge is even better.

Cook the noodles according to the instructions on the package, drain, and refresh under cold water.

In a hot wok, heat 1 tablespoon of the oil, season the tofu, and fry, turning, until golden brown all over, about 2 minutes. Remove and let cool. Add the peanuts to the hot oil and stir-fry until golden brown, about 30 seconds, then set aside to drain on a few paper towels.

Wipe the wok clean with paper towels, reheat, then add the remaining oil. Drain and reserve the marinade from the pork. Add the garlic to the wok and stir-fry for a few seconds. Add the meat and stir-fry for 1 minute to seal. Add the onion to the wok and continue cooking until soft and just beginning to color, about 2 to 3 minutes. Add the chile and stir-fry for 30 seconds. Add the noodles, bean sprouts, Chinese chives, and half the peanuts. Add the dark soy sauce and reserved marinade and continue cooking for another 3 minutes.

Thinly slice the tofu into 4 and add, tossing gently so that the tofu doesn't break up too much. Serve scattered with the remaining peanuts and the cilantro leaves.

3½ ounces rice vermicelli

3 tablespoons vegetable oil

2 teaspoons finely chopped
    shallots

1 garlic clove, peeled and thinly
    sliced

½-inch piece of fresh ginger, peeled
    and finely chopped

1½ ounces pork tenderloin,
    julienned

pinch of crushed red pepper

2 shiitake mushrooms, sliced

1 tablespoon soy sauce

3 ounces raw, peeled shrimp,
    deveined and halved lengthwise

½ teaspoon sugar

1 large egg, lightly beaten

½ cup bean sprouts

2 ounces (about ¼ cup) canned
    chestnuts, drained, rinsed and
    roughly chopped

2 scallions, green parts
    included, finely sliced

cilantro leaves

pork, shrimp, and mushroom noodles

Cook the vermicelli according to the instructions on the package, drain, and refresh under cold water.

Heat the oil in a hot wok. When almost smoking, add the shallots, garlic, and ginger and stir-fry for 1 minute, then add the pork, crushed red pepper, and mushrooms. Stir-fry for another 2 minutes, then add the soy sauce. Add the shrimp and stir-fry for another minute.

Add 2 tablespoons water, the sugar, and the egg. Stir-fry so the egg just cooks and remove from the heat. Add in the noodles, bean sprouts, and chestnuts and top with the scallions and cilantro.

spiced beef noodles

serves 2

7 ounces *udon* noodles

7 ounces beef (boneless top loin
    or sirloin steak), cut into strips
    ¼ inch thick

1 tablespoon cornstarch

salt and white pepper

2 tablespoons vegetable oil

1¼-inch piece of fresh ginger,
    peeled and grated

4 handfuls of baby spinach

2 scallions, cut into
    1½-inch lengths

1 tablespoon soy sauce

1 red chile, seeded and
    finely sliced

2 teaspoons toasted sesame oil

1 teaspoon sesame seed, briefly
    toasted in a hot, dry skillet

Cook the noodles according to the instructions on the package, drain, and refresh under cold water.

Put the beef, cornstarch, and salt and pepper in a plastic food bag and toss the meat to coat. Set aside.

In a hot wok, heat the vegetable oil, add the ginger, and cook for 30 seconds. Add the beef and stir-fry until it is just cooked, about 2 minutes.

Add the spinach, scallions and 1 tablespoon water and toss for 1 minute so that everything is just wilted. Add the soy sauce and chile. Taste and adjust the seasoning. Add the noodles, toss to ensure that everything is combined, and top with the toasted sesame oil and sesame seed.

hot and sour beef ramen

serve 2

3 ounces *ramen* noodles

5 ounces beef tenderloin

2 garlic cloves, peeled and minced

1 red chile, thinly sliced

1 tablespoon rice vinegar

1 tablespoon soy sauce

2¾ cups chicken stock (see
    page 13) or beef stock

½ small red onion, peeled and
    thinly sliced

2 handfuls of bean sprouts

2 teaspoons toasted sesame oil

1 teaspoon sesame seed, briefly
    toasted in a hot, dry skillet

Cook the noodles according to the instructions on the package, drain, and refresh under cold water. Slice the beef as thinly as possible.

In a large saucepan, put the garlic, chile, rice vinegar, and soy sauce with the stock. Bring to a boil, simmer for 2 minutes, then add the beef and cook for a scant minute.

Add the noodles and swirl everything about. Top with the red onion, bean sprouts, and toasted sesame oil and seed, and serve.

stir-fried chili beef with broccoli

serves 2

for the marinade

1 red chile, seeded and sliced

1¼-inch piece of fresh ginger,
    peeled and grated

1 garlic clove, peeled and sliced

½ teaspoon sugar

finely grated zest and juice of
    1 lime

2 teaspoons cornstarch

1 tablespoon vegetable oil

7 ounces beef (boneless sirloin
    steak), trimmed of any
    fat and cut into thin strips

3½ ounces medium egg noodles

2¼ cups small broccoli florets

salt and white pepper

2 tablespoons vegetable oil

1 tablespoon finely sliced shallots

1 tablespoon *mirin* (see page 11)

1 teaspoon fish sauce (*nam pla*)

soy sauce

½ teaspoon sesame seed, briefly
    toasted in a hot, dry skillet

In a medium bowl, combine the marinade ingredients, add the steak, and toss well to combine. Cover and set aside for at least 1 hour; overnight in the fridge is even better.

Cook the noodles according to the instructions on the package, drain, and refresh under cold water.

In a saucepan, blanch the broccoli in boiling salted water until just cooked, about 2–3 minutes. Drain and refresh under cold water.

In a hot wok, heat the oil over high heat and stir-fry the shallots until they just start to color, about 30 seconds. Add the beef and its marinade and continue to cook for another 2 minutes. Add the noodles, broccoli, *mirin,* fish sauce, and 1 tablespoon soy sauce and continue to stir-fry until the meat is cooked and everything is heated through, about another 2 minutes. Season to taste with salt and pepper and soy sauce.

Sprinkle with the sesame seed and serve.

noodles for children

Children love noodles. They are so easygoing (the noodles that is). You can eat, slurp, and suck, use chopsticks, fingers or a fork. The noodles don't mind and nor do the children. As adults these things seem to matter—sort of. But children see beyond that. It is a good partnership.

Noodles are not fussy; they just know what they like. A similarity there from the start. Children get on with things and noodles like that. There is an honesty, an immediacy, which is refreshing. Why make a big fuss over something when there is no need to? What is a noodle other than food? And rather a nice one at that.

The recipes in this chapter tend to be short and stick to easy ingredients, the kind that children tell us they like. This makes them easy to cook, so if the occasion allows, your children can join in too. It is bonding of the best kind. Getting to know your food is, after all, a sure way of feeling involved. Which makes saying yes, or yum for that matter, so much easier.

Short ingredient lists still mean the rather more complex tastes of soy sauce and ginger, garlic and sesame can come into play. Perhaps in muted form. The idea is to encourage exploration. A sense of adventure.

We've tried to keep things simple in this chapter. A kind of introduction. On the basis that enthusiasm and experience is likely to lead to a sense of adventure when other chapters can play a role. After all, children never stay the same. At least that is what we have found.

spring salad with toasted sesame seed

serves 2

for the dressing

2 tablespoons *mirin* (see page 11)
2 tablespoons rice vinegar
2 tablespoons oyster sauce
1 tablespoon sweet chili sauce
1 garlic clove, peeled and minced
1¼-inch piece of fresh ginger,
    peeled and grated

3½ ounces rice vermicelli
small handful of snow peas
1 tablespoon fresh peas, cooked
½ red bell pepper, seeded and cut
    into short, fine slices
1 small zucchini, thinly sliced
4 radishes, thinly sliced
handful of baby spinach leaves
salt and white pepper
2 teaspoons sesame seed, briefly
    toasted in a hot, dry skillet

Cook the vermicelli according to the instructions on the package, drain, and refresh briefly under cold water. Roughly chop.

In a large bowl, combine the dressing ingredients and toss the warm vermicelli through.

Add the snow peas, peas, red pepper, zucchini, radishes, and spinach to the noodles and toss to ensure that everything is well combined. Taste and season with salt and pepper.

Serve sprinkled with the sesame seed.

lightly curried vegetable noodles

serves 2

5 ounces thin white *somen* noodles
1 tablespoon vegetable oil
1 red onion, peeled and thinly sliced
1 red bell pepper, seeded
    and sliced
½ Chinese cabbage, thinly sliced
8 button mushrooms, thinly sliced
1 tablespoon *kare lomen* sauce
    (see page 21)
1 tablespoon soy sauce
salt and white pepper
½ teaspoon sugar
½ teaspoon *dashi no moto*
    (see page 11)
handful of bean sprouts
bunch of cilantro, leaves picked
¼ cucumber, seeded and
    julienned

Cook the noodles according to the instructions on the package, drain, and refresh under cold water.

In a hot wok, heat the vegetable oil over medium–high heat and stir-fry the red onion, red bell pepper, cabbage, and mushrooms for 2 minutes. Add the *kare lomen* sauce and stir-fry until the mixture starts to color and the aroma becomes sweet and rounded, about 5 minutes. Add the soy sauce, ⅔ cup water, season with salt and pepper, add the sugar and *dashi no moto*, and simmer for 1 minute.

Divide the noodles between 2 bowls and spoon over the vegetables. Serve topped with the bean sprouts, cilantro and cucumber.

thai-style shrimp and fried noodles

serves 4 small ones

3½ ounces wide rice noodles
1 tablespoon vegetable oil
1 garlic clove, peeled and finely
    chopped
2 lemongrass stalks, outer leaves
    removed, finely chopped
1 large egg, beaten and seasoned
5 ounces raw, peeled shrimp,
    deveined
1 tablespoon fish sauce (nam pla)
1 teaspoon brown sugar
2 teaspoons soy sauce
large handful of roasted peanuts,
    coarsely chopped
handful of bean sprouts
small bunch of cilantro, leaves picked
salt and white pepper

Cook the noodles according to the instructions on the package, drain, and refresh under cold water.

In a hot wok, heat the oil and stir-fry the garlic and lemongrass for 30 seconds. Add the egg, swirl it around for 30 seconds, then add the noodles, shrimp, fish sauce, sugar, soy sauce, and half the peanuts. Stir-fry to cook the shrimp, about 2 minutes.

Add the bean sprouts and cilantro, check the seasoning, and toss to ensure that everything is heated through, about 1 minute.

Serve with the remaining peanuts scattered over the top.

stir-fried shrimp and peas

serves 4 small ones

5 ounces thin egg noodles
1 tablespoon vegetable oil
1 garlic clove, peeled and finely
    chopped
½-inch piece of fresh ginger, peeled
    and finely chopped
5 ounces raw, peeled shrimp,
    deveined
3 tablespoons frozen peas,
    defrosted
1 tablespoon soy sauce
1 teaspoon cornstarch, dissolved in
    2 tablespoons water
⅔ cup chicken stock (see
    page 13)
salt and white pepper

Cook the noodles according to the instructions on the package, drain, and refresh under cold water.

In a hot wok, heat the oil and add the garlic and ginger. Toss and then add the shrimp and stir-fry for 1 minute. Add the peas and cook for another minute, then add the noodles, soy sauce, dissolved cornstarch and chicken stock. Season with salt and pepper and cook to ensure that everything is heated through, then serve.

4½ ounces medium egg noodles

2 teaspoons vegetable oil

1 tablespoon red curry paste
    (see page 16)

1 tablespoon coconut milk

juice of 1 lime

2 teaspoons fish sauce (*nam pla*)

2 teaspoons finely chopped
    shallots

1 pound mussels, scrubbed and
    debearded

handful of spinach leaves

salt and white pepper

thai-style mussels with egg noodles

Cook the noodles according to the instructions on the package, drain, and refresh under cold water.

In a hot wok with a lid (or a large lidded saucepan), heat the oil and stir-fry the curry paste, coconut milk, lime juice, fish sauce, and shallots for 3 minutes, ensuring the mixture doesn't catch. You want the curry paste to lose its raw aroma.

Add the mussels and toss so that everything is well combined. Cover, reduce the heat, and cook, shaking the pan occasionally, until all the mussels open, about 5 minutes. Discard any mussels that remain closed.

Remove the lid, stir in the drained noodles and spinach, and check the seasoning. Cook until the noodles are heated through and the spinach just wilted, about 1 minute. Serve.

stir-fried chicken and sweetcorn

serves 4 small ones

3½ ounces medium egg noodles

1 tablespoon vegetable oil

1 garlic clove, peeled and finely
    chopped

3½ ounces chicken thigh meat, cut
    into bite-size pieces

handful of snow peas, thinly sliced
    lengthwise

1 tablespoon soy sauce

2 teaspoons fish sauce (*nam pla*)

1 cup canned corn, drained

salt and white pepper

2 teaspoons sesame seed, briefly
    toasted in a hot, dry skillet

1 teaspoon toasted sesame oil

bunch of cilantro, leaves picked

Cook the noodles according to the instructions on the package, drain, and refresh under cold water.

In a hot wok, heat the vegetable oil and stir-fry the garlic for 30 seconds. Add the chicken, and continue to stir-fry until the meat is cooked, about 3 to 4 minutes. Add the snow peas, soy sauce, and fish sauce and simmer for 30 seconds before adding the noodles and corn. Season with salt and pepper and continue to cook for 1 minute.

Remove from the heat, add the sesame seed and sesame oil, and toss to coat everything well.

Serve scattered with the cilantro.

3½ ounces wide rice noodles
1 tablespoon vegetable oil
1 garlic clove, peeled and finely
  chopped
1¼-inch piece of fresh ginger root,
  peeled and grated
7 ounces beef (boneless top loin
  steak), cut into thin strips
1 medium carrot, julienned
handful of snow peas, sliced thinly
  lengthwise
zest and juice of 1 orange
1 tablespoon soy sauce
2 teaspoons oyster sauce
1 tablespoon toasted sesame oil
handful of bean sprouts
salt and white pepper
1 tablespoon sesame seed, briefly
  toasted in a hot, dry skillet

serves 4 small ones

for the marinade
1¼-inch piece of fresh ginger,
  peeled and grated
1 garlic clove, peeled and minced
zest and juice of 1 orange
1 tablespoon soy sauce
1 tablespoon dark brown sugar

7 ounces dark chicken meat
  (leg or thigh), roughly chopped
5 ounces medium egg noodles
1 tablespoon vegetable oil
handful of snow peas, thinly sliced
¾ cup baby corn, halved lengthwise
⅓ cup chicken stock (see page 13)
1 tablespoon cornstarch
1 tablespoon toasted sesame oil
1 tablespoon sesame seed, briefly
  toasted in a hot, dry frying pan
1 lime, quartered

beef and orange stir-fry

Cook the noodles according to the instructions on the package, drain, and refresh under cold water.

In a hot wok, heat the oil and stir-fry the garlic and ginger for 30 seconds. Add the beef and carrot and stir-fry for 3 minutes. Add the snow peas and continue to stir-fry for 1 minute. Add the orange zest and juice, soy sauce, oyster sauce, sesame oil, and bean sprouts. Add the noodles and toss to ensure that everything is well coated and heated through. Check the seasoning.

Serve with a scattering of sesame seed.

marinated chicken with orange, soy sauce and ginger

In a small saucepan, combine the marinade ingredients and gently heat to dissolve the sugar. Let cool and add the chicken, toss so that it is well coated, and set aside for at least 1 hour; overnight in the fridge is even better.

Cook the noodles according to the instructions on the package, drain, and refresh under cold water.

In a hot wok, heat the oil, add the chicken (reserve the marinade), and stir-fry until golden, about 2 to 3 minutes. Add the snow peas, baby corn, reserved marinade, and chicken stock and continue to stir-fry until the chicken is cooked and the vegetables are just wilting, about 2 minutes. Dissolve the cornstarch in 1 tablespoon water, add to the wok, and simmer until thickened, about 1 minute.

Add the noodles and toss through, along with the sesame oil, to ensure everything is well coated and heated through.

Serve scattered with the sesame seed and with a lime wedge.

salads

Cold noodles? What a thought. Yet this is common throughout Asia and has been for centuries. A Sunday treat in Japan is ice-cold buckwheat noodles and soy dipping sauce. Surprisingly good.

This chapter is full of cold noodles. Dressed, along with other ingredients, is a pretty good definition of a salad. On a hot day what can be more yummy than the chilled tingle of ginger and soy with crunchy vegetables. Refreshing too. The same is true of fish. Think of an Italian seafood salad with potatoes and you get the idea. Only with noodles you get added slurp.

A salad is a good contrast in any assembly of dishes. Some might say a little light relief. We like to think of noodle salads as rather more important than that. A difference with attitude. The noodles that bring flavor—like *somen*— are quite a surprise really. Chilling a noodle does rather a lot for its character. Sort of draws it out. So what might add crunch—as beanthreads do—reveals rather a clean, delicate flavor when eaten cold. All the other noodles, wheat and rice, come across with surprising flavor profiles. But then, served cold, so do quite a lot of other ingredients. Lettuce for instance. And peas. And all this is before you consider your dressing. And seasoning.

Your dressing is what brings everything together. It must perform however. *Nam pla* (fish sauce) might seem an odd ingredient to put in a dressing, but its sourness works wonders. Lime juice adds acidity. Soy an unmistakable zest. Sesame oil brings a rich nuttiness. Sugar a sweetness. Combined and in the right proportion you have a kind of happiness. The kind you want to eat.

spinach and potato noodle salad

serves 2

1 medium potato, peeled and cut
    into 1¼-inch cubes
salt and white pepper
3½ ounces cellophane noodles
2 tablespoons vegetable oil
1 tablespoon finely chopped shallots
½ teaspoon turmeric
1 tablespoon fish sauce (*nam pla*)
1 tablespoon toasted sesame oil
2 handfuls of baby spinach leaves
finely grated zest and juice of
    1 lemon

Put the potatoes in cold, salted water, bring to a boil, and simmer until tender, about 8 minutes.

Soften the noodles according to the instructions on the package, drain, and refresh under cold water.

In a hot wok, heat the oil and stir-fry the shallots and turmeric until golden brown, about 1 to 2 minutes. Add the fish sauce, remove from the heat, and stir in the noodles and sesame oil. Transfer to a bowl.

Drain the potatoes and toss through gently to ensure that everything is heated through. Add the spinach and lemon zest and juice, toss again, check the seasoning, and serve.

rice noodle salad

serves 2

2 ounces medium rice noodles
¼ cup frozen peas
2 scallions, finely sliced
6 radishes, finely sliced
2-inch piece of cucumber, cut
    into half-moon slices
small handful of bean sprouts
1 red chile (or to taste),
    seeded and finely sliced
small handful of snow peas,
    finely sliced
2 teaspoons fish sauce (*nam pla*)
1 teaspoon brown sugar
1 teaspoon soy sauce
finely grated zest and juice of
    1 lime
½-inch piece of ginger root, peeled
    and grated
1 garlic clove, peeled and
    finely sliced
toasted sesame oil
salt and white pepper
2 tablespoons chopped cilantro
2 teaspoons roughly chopped
    roasted peanuts

Cook the noodles according to the instructions on the package, drain, and refresh under cold water.

Cook the peas for 1 minute in boiling unsalted water, then plunge into cold water. When cold, in a large bowl, toss with the other prepared vegetables and the noodles.

In a small saucepan, combine the fish sauce, sugar, and soy sauce and heat until the sugar just dissolves. Add the lime zest and juice, ginger, and garlic and 1 tablespoon sesame oil. Pour over the noodle mixture, toss well, season with salt and pepper, and add more sesame oil to taste.

Serve scattered with the cilantro leaves and peanuts.

soba noodle salad

serves 2

for the dressing

1 teaspoon honey
1 teaspoon fish sauce (*nam pla*)
1 teaspoon rice vinegar
1 teaspoon *mirin* (see page 11)

3½ ounces *soba* noodles
finely grated zest and juice of
    1 lime
8 radishes, thinly sliced
½ cucumber, seeded and
    finely sliced
1 carrot, peeled and julienned
bunch of mint, leaves roughly chopped
2 handfuls of spinach, roughly
    chopped
salt and white pepper

Cook the noodles according to the instructions on the package, drain, and refresh under cold water.

In a small saucepan, mix together the dressing ingredients, bring to a boil, and set aside to cool. Stir in the lime zest and juice.

In a large bowl, combine the noodles with the radishes, cucumber, carrot, mint, and spinach, add the cooled dressing, and toss to ensure that everything is coated. Check the seasoning and serve.

summer salad with pickled ginger

serves 2

3½ ounces rice vermicelli
bunch of asparagus spears, woody
    ends removed
salt
1 tablespoon vegetable oil
2 eggs, beaten and seasoned
½ cucumber, julienned
1 carrot, peeled and julienned
handful of bean sprouts
1 red chile, seeded and sliced
handful of mint leaves
1 sheet of *nori* seaweed,
    roughly torn
1 teaspoon sesame seed

for the dressing

2 teaspoons soy sauce
2 teaspoons pickled ginger, roughly
    chopped
1 teaspoon fish sauce (*nam pla*)
2 teaspoons *mirin* (see page 11)
juice of 1 lime

Cook the vermicelli according to the instructions on the package, drain, and refresh in cold water. Roughly chop.

Cook the asparagus in boiling salted water until just tender, about 3 to 5 minutes (depending on thickness). Drain and refresh in cold water and cut in half.

In a hot wok, heat the oil, then add the egg, swirl around so that it thinly coats the bottom of the wok, and cook until set, about 1 minute. Remove, let cool, then roll up and thinly slice.

In a large bowl, combine the egg, noodles, and asparagus with the cucumber, carrot, bean sprouts, and chile.

Mix together the dressing ingredients and add to the salad.

Transfer to a plate and serve scattered with the mint leaves, *nori*, and sesame seed.

pickled vegetable noodles

serves 2

2 teaspoons *mirin* (see page 11)

2 teaspoons soy sauce

2 teaspoons toasted sesame oil

pinch of sugar

1 garlic clove, peeled and crushed

3½ ounces (scant ½ cup) *kimchee* (see page 11), roughly chopped, juices reserved

1 cucumber, shaved into long, thin strips with a vegetable peeler

1 red onion, peeled and thinly sliced

2 carrots, peeled and julienned

5 ounces *somen* noodles

1 teaspoon sesame seed, briefly toasted in a hot, dry skillet

2 teaspoons roughly chopped roasted peanuts

In a large bowl, combine the *mirin,* soy sauce, sesame oil, and sugar with the garlic and stir in the *kimchee*. Add the cucumber, red onion, and carrots. Toss gently to coat everything with dressing and set aside.

Cook the noodles according to the instructions on the package, drain, and refresh under cold water.

Add the noodles, sesame seed, and reserved *kimchee* juices to the salad and toss to ensure that everything is well coated.

Serve topped with the chopped peanuts.

mushroom salad with somen noodles

serves 2

1 heaping cup button mushrooms, quartered

1 tablespoon rice vinegar

2 garlic cloves, peeled and minced

bunch of cilantro, leaves picked, stems finely chopped

2 tablespoons vegetable oil

1 tablespoon toasted sesame oil

3 ounces *somen* noodles

1 tablespoon soy sauce

1 tablespoon sweet dipping chili sauce (see page 16)

4 scallions, finely sliced

2 heads of Bibb lettuce, finely sliced

1 carrot, peeled and cut into matchsticks

bunch of mint, roughly chopped

1 lime, halved

In a saucepan, combine the mushrooms with the rice vinegar, garlic, cilantro stems, vegetable oil, sesame oil, and 2 tablespoons water. Cover and simmer, stirring occasionally, until the mushrooms have wilted but retain some bite, about 8 to 10 minutes. Let cool.

Cook the noodles according to the instructions on the package, drain, and refresh under cold water.

In a large bowl, combine the noodles with the soy sauce, sweet chili sauce, scallions, lettuce, carrot, mint, and reserved cilantro leaves. Add the mushrooms and their juices and toss to ensure that everything is well coated.

Serve with the lime halves.

1 teaspoon light brown sugar

2 teaspoons fish sauce (*nam pla*)

juice of 1 lime

1 tablespoon vegetable oil

12 cooked, peeled shrimp, deveined

3½ ounces cellophane noodles

6 asparagus spears, cut into 1½-inch lengths

¼ cucumber, seeded and julienned

6 radishes, finely sliced

1 red chile (or to taste), seeded and finely chopped

1 garlic clove, peeled and finely chopped

2 scallions, finely sliced

small bunch of cilantro, leaves picked, stems finely chopped

2 teaspoons sesame seed, briefly toasted in a hot, dry skillet

shrimp, asparagus, and noodle salad

In a medium bowl, combine the sugar, fish sauce, lime juice, and vegetable oil and toss the shrimp through.

Cook the noodles according to the instructions on the package, drain, and refresh under cold water.

In a saucepan, cook the asparagus in boiling salted water until just tender, about 3 to 5 minutes (depending on thickness), drain, and refresh under cold water. In a large bowl, combine the asparagus with the cucumber, radishes, and noodles. Add the chile, garlic, scallions, and cilantro stems.

Add the shrimp mixture to the noodles and toss everything so that it is well coated. Serve with a generous sprinkling of the reserved cilantro leaves and sesame seed.

If you buy raw shrimp for a salad like this, it is best to cook the shrimp gently, starting them in cold salted water, bringing them to a boil and simmering for a couple of minutes, before draining and peeling. This way the flesh stays moist and succulent.

seafood salad
with wilted greens

serves 2

for the dressing
1 tablespoon toasted sesame oil
2 tablespoons soy sauce
1/2 teaspoon sugar
2 tablespoons rice vinegar
2 scallions, finely sliced
1 1/4-inch piece of fresh ginger,
    peeled and grated
2 garlic cloves, peeled and minced
    with a little salt

3 1/2 ounces cellophane noodles
1 small head of Bibb lettuce,
    trimmed and shredded
small handful of snow peas, thinly
    sliced lengthwise
small handful of bean sprouts
1/4 cucumber, seeded and
    julienned
1 tablespoon vegetable oil
4 sea scallops, shelled and trimmed
    (if large, slice horizontally)
4 raw, peeled shrimp, deveined
8 small clams, well rinsed and
    drained
handful of spinach
bunch of cilantro, leaves picked

Soak the noodles according to the instructions on the package, drain, and refresh under cold water. Roughly chop and put in a large bowl.

Combine the dressing ingredients and stir to dissolve the sugar. Add to the bowl along with with the lettuce, snow peas, bean sprouts, and cucumber, toss well, and check the seasoning. In a hot wok, heat the oil in a hot wok over medium heat and stir-fry the scallops, shrimp, and clams until cooked and the clams are open, about 2 minutes.

Add the spinach, wilt briefly over the heat, and add everything to the salad bowl. Toss well, adding in the cilantro as you go, and serve.

kamaboko-aka salad

serves 2

3 1/2 ounces cellophane noodles
1 whole red *kamaboko-aka* (see
    page 11), sliced
1 celery stalk, thinly sliced
1 tablespoon finely sliced shallots
handful of bean sprouts
1 small head of Bibb lettuce, leaves
    separated
1 teaspoon fish sauce (*nam pla*)
1 teaspoon soy sauce
salt and white pepper

Cook the noodles according to the instructions on the package, drain, and refresh under cold water.

In a large bowl, combine the *kamaboko-aka*, celery, shallots, bean sprouts, lettuce, noodles, fish sauce, and soy sauce. Season with salt and pepper and toss well before serving.

somen noodle salad with scallops and kamaboko-aka

serves 2

for the dressing

½ cup soy sauce

½ cup rice vinegar

1 teaspoon toasted sesame oil

1 teaspoon sugar

3½ ounces *somen* noodles

1 small head of Bibb lettuce,
    trimmed and shredded

½ cucumber, cut into strips using a
    vegetable peeler

½ red bell pepper, sliced lengthwise

1 sheet of *nori* seaweed, cut into
    ½-inch strips

2 scallions, finely sliced

1 tablespoon vegetable oil

salt and white pepper

6 sea scallops, shelled, trimmed
    and sliced in half horizontally

½ *kamaboko-aka* (see page 11),
    cut into ⅟₁₆-inch slices

1 teaspoon sesame seeds, briefly
    toasted in a hot, dry skillet

Combine the dressing ingredients in a small bowl.

Cook the noodles according to the instructions on the package, drain, and refresh under cold water.

In a large bowl, combine half the dressing (keep the rest in the fridge for other salads or to serve over noodle dishes; it will last a week or so) with the lettuce, cucumber, red bell pepper, *nori,* scallions, and noodles and toss well. Transfer to a plate.

In a hot wok, heat the vegetable oil. Season the scallops, and fry until cooked through, about 1 to 2 minutes. Place on top of the salad ingredients along with the *kamaboko-aka* slices and a sprinkling of sesame seed.

shrimp and rice vermicelli salad

serves 2

3½ ounces rice vermicelli

7 ounces raw, peeled shrimp,
    deveined

1¼-inch piece of ginger root,
    peeled and grated

2 garlic cloves, peeled and minced

1 tablespoon fish sauce (*nam pla*)

2 tablespoons vegetable oil

bunch of chives, cut into 2½-inch
    lengths

1 red chile, finely chopped

handful of bean sprouts

2 tablespoons sweet *miso* dressing
    (see page 23)

bunch of cilantro, leaves picked

1 tablespoon sesame seed, briefly
    toasted in a hot, dry skillet

Cook the vermicelli according to the instructions on the package, drain, and refresh under cold water.

In a medium bowl, toss the shrimp with the ginger, garlic, and fish sauce.

In a hot wok, heat the oil over medium heat, add the shrimp mixture, and stir-fry until the shrimp are cooked, about 2 to 3 minutes. Add the noodles, chives, chile, and bean sprouts and immediately remove from the heat.

Stir in the sweet *miso* dressing and serve topped with the cilantro leaves and sesame seed.

mango, shrimp, and crab noodle salad

serves 2

for the dressing

1¼-inch piece of ginger root,
    peeled and grated
2 garlic cloves, peeled and sliced
juice of 1 lime
1 tablespoon vegetable oil
½ teaspoon sugar
1 tablespoon fish sauce (*nam pla*)
1 tablespoon soy sauce

3½ ounces rice noodles
1 mango, pitted, peeled and
    roughly chopped
2 tablespoons cooked lump
    crabmeat
5 ounces cooked, peeled shrimp
small bunch of mint, leaves roughly
    chopped
salt and white pepper

Cook the noodles according to the instructions on the package, drain, and refresh under cold water.

In a large bowl, combine the dressing ingredients. Mix in the noodles and toss to ensure that everything is well combined.

Stir in the mango, crabmeat, shrimp, and mint, check the seasoning, and serve.

marinated sea bass salad

serves 2

3½ ounces cellophane noodles
½ pound sea bass (branzini) fillets,
    skinned
1 tablespoon vegetable oil
salt
2 tablespoons *tori kara age* sauce
    (see page 21)
leaves of 1 small head of Bibb
    lettuce
handful of bean sprouts
3 scallions, finely sliced
handful of baby spinach
¼ cucumber, seeded and
    julienned
1 tablespoon chopped mint leaves
1 garlic clove, peeled and thinly
    sliced
¾-inch piece of ginger root, peeled
    and julienned
1 tablespoon soy sauce
1 lime, halved

Soak the noodles according to the instructions on the package, drain, and refresh under cold water.

Cut the sea bass into bite-size pieces. Toss with the oil, season with salt, and cook on a hot grill or under a broiler until just cooked, 3 to 4 minutes. Remove and transfer to a bowl. Add the *tori kara age* sauce and set aside for 5 minutes.

In a large bowl, combine the noodles, lettuce, bean sprouts, scallions, spinach, cucumber, mint, garlic, ginger, and soy sauce. Toss to ensure that everything is well combined and divide between 2 bowls. Top with the fish and its sauce and serve with a lime half.

warm chicken teriyaki salad

serves 2

for the marinade

2 tablespoons sake

2 tablespoons *mirin* (see page 11)

2 tablespoons soy sauce

1 teaspoon light brown sugar

1¼-inch piece of ginger root,
    peeled and grated

2 garlic cloves, peeled and finely
    chopped

7 ounces dark chicken meat (leg or
    thigh), roughly chopped

3½ ounces rice vermicelli

2 teaspoons toasted sesame oil

1 tablespoon vegetable oil

2 handfuls of bean sprouts

1 small head of Bibb lettuce, leaves
    separated and shredded

1 red chile, seeded and finely
    chopped

4 tablespoons frozen peas,
    defrosted

bunch of cilantro, leaves picked

salt and white pepper

1 tablespoon coarsely chopped
    salted peanuts

In a saucepan, combine the marinade ingredients and gently heat to dissolve the sugar. Let cool completely, then combine with the chicken. Cover and set aside for 1 hour; overnight in the fridge is even better.

Cook the vermicelli according to the instructions on the package, drain, and refresh under cold water. Toss with the sesame oil.

In a hot wok, heat the vegetable oil over medium heat and add the chicken and its marinade. Cook until the meat is done and the liquid is reduced and thickened, about 4 minutes. Remove from the heat.

In a large bowl, combine the noodles with the bean sprouts, lettuce, chile, peas, and cilantro leaves. Season with salt and pepper and toss to ensure that everything is well mixed.

Pile on to 2 plates, spoon over the chicken and its juices, and serve topped with the peanuts.

chicken sesame noodles

serves 2

3½ ounces medium egg noodles
1 tablespoon toasted sesame oil

for the dressing
2 garlic cloves
½-inch piece of fresh ginger, peeled
     and grated
1 tablespoon toasted sesame oil
1 tablespoon soy sauce
1 tablespoon rice vinegar
1 teaspoon Chinese black vinegar
     (available from Asian markets)
1 teaspoon light brown sugar

3½ ounces cooked chicken breast,
     cut into finger-sized strips
½ cucumber, cut lengthwise into
     strips using a vegetable peeler
4 radishes, sliced
2 handfuls of bean sprouts
2 scallions, thinly sliced
1 tablespoon sesame seed, briefly
     toasted in a hot, dry skillet

Cook the noodles according to the instructions on the package, drain, and refresh under cold water. Toss with the sesame oil and set aside.

In a large bowl, combine the dressing ingredients and stir in the chicken.

Toss the chicken and dressing with the noodles and scatter over the cucumber, radishes, bean sprouts, scallions, and sesame seed.

3½ ounces green beans, trimmed
    and cut into 4cm lengths
salt and white pepper
1 red bell pepper, seeded and
    thinly sliced
2 skinless, boneless chicken
    breasts
3½ ounces rice noodles
juice of 2 limes
2 teaspoons light brown sugar
2 tablespoons soy sauce
⅓ cup fresh mango, cut into
    ½-inch cubes
small bunch of mint, leaves
    picked and roughly chopped
½ cup roughly chopped roasted,
    salted peanuts

chicken and mango rice noodle salad

Bring a large saucepan of salted water to a boil and cook the beans until just tender, about 4 minutes. Add the red bell pepper and return to a boil. Lift out immediately using a slotted spoon and refresh under cold water. Drain well and set aside.

Slide the chicken breasts into the same pan of boiling water, reduce the heat, and simmer until cooked, about 6 to 8 minutes. Remove the chicken and let cool. Slice into bite-size pieces.

Add the noodles to the boiling water and cook according to the instructions on the package, drain, and refresh under cold water.

In a large bowl, whisk together the lime juice and sugar until the sugar dissolves, then add the soy sauce. Stir in the vegetables, noodles, chicken, mango, and mint.

Season with salt and pepper and toss everything lightly to dress all the ingredients. Taste and adjust the seasoning as required.

Serve with the peanuts scattered over the top.

serves 2

3½ ounces *somen* noodles
2 teaspoons tahini paste
1¼-inch piece of fresh ginger,
    peeled and grated
1 small jalapeño chile, seeded
    and finely chopped
2 teaspoons soy sauce
2 teaspoons rice vinegar
1 tablespoon vegetable oil
salt and white pepper
3½ ounces boneless chicken thigh
    meat, roughly chopped
1 small head of Bibb lettuce, leaves
    finely shredded
½ cucumber, cut lengthwise into
    strips using a vegetable peeler
handful of mint leaves
handful of cilantro leaves

chicken and cilantro somen noodles

Cook the noodles according to the instructions on the package, drain, and refresh under cold water.

In a small bowl, combine the tahini paste, ginger, and chile with the soy sauce and rice vinegar.

In a hot wok, heat the oil, season the chicken, and stir-fry until golden brown and cooked through. Add the tahini sauce and stir in 2 tablespoons warm water. Combine the chicken, sauce, noodles, lettuce, cucumber, mint, and cilantro. Check the seasoning and serve.

marinated duck salad

serves 2

for the marinade
1 teaspoon rice vinegar
1 teaspoon honey
1 teaspoon soy sauce

1 boneless duck breast, sliced on
    the diagonal
1 tablespoon vegetable oil
7 ounces *somen* noodles
bunch of scallions, sliced
    lengthwise
½ cucumber, seeded and
    julienned
1 carrot, peeled and julienned
2 tablespoons hoisin sauce
salt and white pepper
2 teaspoons sesame seed, briefly
    toasted in a hot, dry skillet

In a small saucepan, combine the marinade ingredients with ⅓ cup cold water, bring to a boil, and remove from the heat as soon as the honey has melted. Let cool completely and pour over the duck slices in a dish. Toss gently, cover, and set aside for 1 hour; overnight in the fridge is even better.

Pour the marinade off the duck and discard. In a hot wok, heat the oil and stir-fry the duck until cooked, 3 to 4 minutes. Set aside.

Cook the noodles according to the instructions on the package, drain, and refresh under cold water.

In a large bowl, combine the noodles with the scallions, cucumber, carrot, and hoisin sauce. Add the duck and toss everything gently so that it is well mixed and coated. Season to taste with salt and pepper.

Serve topped with the sesame seed.

chicken noodle salad

serves 2

2 ounces rice vermicelli
1 tablespoon vegetable oil
1¼-inch piece of ginger root,
    peeled and grated
2 teaspoons soy sauce
finely grated zest and juice of
    1 lime
2 teaspoons toasted sesame oil
3 ounces cooked chicken breast,
    sliced
1 small head of Bibb lettuce,
    finely sliced
1 red chile, seeded and finely sliced
2 scallions, thinly sliced
handful of bean sprouts
½ cucumber, seeded and finely
    sliced
1 tablespoon roughly chopped
    roasted peanuts
handful of cilantro leaves

Cook the vermicelli according to the instructions on the package, drain, and refresh under cold water. Roughly chop.

In a large bowl, combine the vegetable oil with the ginger, soy sauce, lime zest and juice, and the sesame oil. Toss with the noodles. Stir in the chicken, lettuce, chile, scallions, bean sprouts, and cucumber.

Serve topped with the peanuts and cilantro leaves.

for the marinade

2 teaspoons *char siu* sauce
   (Chinese barbecue sauce,
   which is widely available)
1 garlic clove, peeled and finely
   chopped
pinch of Chinese five-spice
   (available from Asian markets)
pinch of ground cinnamon
2 teaspoons sake
2 teaspoons rice vinegar or
   lemon juice

3 ounces pork tenderloin
2 tablespoons vegetable oil
⅔ cup sugar
½ cup soy sauce
½ cup rice vinegar
3½ ounces *somen* noodles
2 large eggs, beaten and seasoned
1 small head of Bibb lettuce, finely
   sliced
⅓ cucumber, seeded and
   thinly sliced
3 scallions, thinly sliced
   on the diagonal
½ roll *kamaboko-aka* (see page 11),
   cut into 1⁄16-inch slices
1 sheet of *nori* seaweed, cut
   into strips
salt and white pepper
1 teaspoon toasted sesame oil
½ teaspoon sesame seeds, briefly
   toasted in a hot, dry skillet
½ teaspoon black sesame seed

marinated pork and somen noodle salad

Put the marinade ingredients in a plastic food bag, add the pork, massage for a few minutes, and transfer to the fridge overnight or for as long as possible.

Preheat the oven to 400°F. Heat a heavy-bottom skillet until hot, add 1 tablespoon of the vegetable oil, and cook the pork in the skillet to seal, rolling it around until golden all over, 2 to 3 minutes. Transfer to a roasting pan and roast until cooked, 20 minutes. Remove and let rest for 5 minutes, then cut into disks ¼-inch thick.

In a small bowl, combine the sugar, soy sauce, and rice vinegar, and stir to dissolve the sugar. This is the dressing.

Cook the noodles according to the instructions on the package, drain, and refresh under cold water.

In a hot wok, heat the remaining oil, then add the egg, swirl around so that it thinly coats the bottom of the wok, and cook until set, about 1 minute. Remove, let cool, then roll up and thinly slice.

To serve, mix together the pork, noodles, egg strips, lettuce, cucumber, scallions, *kamaboko-aka*, and *nori* and place in a serving bowl. Whisk the dressing and pour over 3 tablespoons (the remainder can be stored in an airtight container in the fridge for a few weeks). Toss to ensure that everything is well mixed, season with salt and pepper, drizzle over the sesame oil, and serve with a sprinkling of the sesame seed.

wagamama

drinks

What to drink with noodles is something of a challenge. Consider it more to do with preference than anything else, as noodles are pretty easy really. Tea is popular. Green is favorite, but there is nothing wrong with a straight "cuppa" if that is what you prefer. Many opt for beer— we favor Japanese beers in the restaurants. Juices and smoothies get high marks from customers; it's a health thing. But also a taste thing. Wine works well, although you need to be a bit cautious with the spicier dishes and those where the chile factor is higher, as some wines are more suited than others. Red or white is a matter of choice. Noodles seem to like both. Sake is well worth considering, of which more later. And plain water is rather delicious; ice-cold, it is refreshing and very complementary to a slurp or two. Of noodles as well as of water.

juices and smoothies

Sales of juices and smoothies have increased significantly in recent years, not just at wagamama but generally. Packed with clean pure flavors, the health benefits seem like a bonus point. Some of these drinks are almost like a meal in themselves, which is partly why they sit at the top of the menu. A glass of raw juice (carrot, cucumber, tomato, orange, and apple) is a great way to enjoy the anticipation of a bowl of noodles.

Apart from orange and grapefruit juice, juices are not that easy to produce at home unless you have a proper juice machine. This pulps the fruit or vegetable in order to extract the juice. Smoothies are somewhat easier, although you do have to stick to softer ingredients, like bananas, mangoes, and berries. Most smoothies contain banana, which helps to give the drink some body. There really is no end to the variations of juices possible.

What follows are a couple of suggestions that make use of a blender. If you decide to purchase a juicer, the whole world of vegetables adds a completely different dimension.

serves 1

1 orange, peeled, seeded, and
    all white pith removed
20 seedless red grapes
10 lychees, canned or fresh
10 sprigs of mint

orange, lychee, grape, and mint juice

Place everything in a blender or food processor and blitz on the pulse setting until smooth. Serve immediately.

serves 1

1 small banana, peeled
1 pear, peeled and cored
1 lime, peeled and all white pith
    removed
2 teaspoons honey

banana, pear, honey, and lime smoothie

Place everything in a blender or food processor and blitz on the pulse setting until smooth. Serve immediately.

water

If you opt for spicier dishes, it might be worth avoiding sparkling water, as the bubbles tend to accentuate the chile burn. A still water, from the faucet even, preferably chilled, does much to quench thirst and clear the palate.

tea

We favor green tea over black. It's the tannins really, which in black tea tend to overpower the noodles, if not all the other ingredients. Jasmine is generally overwhelmed by the food. Which leaves green tea sitting rather neatly in the middle. In the world of green teas there are literally hundreds to choose from. To those in the know there are also huge differences. Best to try and see which one you prefer.

serves 2

1½ cups cooked rice
3½ ounces cooked fish, loosely
    flaked
2 cups green tea
1 sheet *nori* seaweed, roughly torn

tea and rice

Pour the tea over the rice and fish, scatter the *nori* on top, and drink/eat/slurp.

This is a popular way of finishing a meal in Japan: tea is poured over leftover rice to make a kind of instant oatmeal. There is a temptation to add other things, as evidenced by the fish in this recipe. A frugal and rather different approach to leftovers.

serves 1

½-inch piece of lemongrass, bashed
1 teaspoon peeled and grated
    fresh ginger
2 teaspoons honey

lemongrass, ginger, and honey infusion

Combine all the ingredients in a small pitcher and pour over a mug of hot water. Let infuse for 5 minutes, strain, and serve.

wine

If it's white you want, stick to something dry, fairly neutral, and fresh (which means a generous but balanced acidity). Aromatic whites are also worth considering. Grape varieties to look out for include Sauvignon Blanc, Pinot Gris, Pinot Blanc, Riesling, and Viognier.

On the red side, watch out for tannins, which come up hard against chiles and anything spicy. Light and fresh is the favored route: Beaujolais, Syrah (provided the tannins are low), wines from the Loire—Chinon, for example—or light Sangiovese and Tempranillo.

Rosé may be a pretty general term in that the wines vary hugely, but on the whole they partner really well, their light fruitiness working harmoniously with the spiciness and the absence of tannins avoiding any clash.

beer

Beer is not quite as easy or obvious as it might at first seem. We have Japanese beers on the menu, because they are dry, not too hoppy and not overly gassy, which makes them good partners with food. They also have some character, which is necessary for them to stand up to the food. Avoid inexpensive lagers, which tend to fall at the first post. But look out for the more interesting lagers, which tend to have lots of character and sufficient alcohol (around 5% abv) to cope with the flavors. The darker beers—ales, porters and stouts—tend to overwhelm the more delicate aspects of the food.

sake

Sake's body, character, aroma, and strength make it very suited to combining with this kind of food. Like fino or manzanilla sherry (both of which are worth trying with noodles), sake is able to handle the chile and spicy notes well. There are many sakes and price is not necessarily a straight indication of, or route to, satisfaction. On the menu we have two, one slightly sweeter than the other. If you are buying a bottle the labeling has become a lot clearer than it used to be. Look out for *nihonshu-do*, an indication of dryness and sweetness. +15 is very dry, −15 is very sweet, with neutral being between −3 and +5. *Sanmi-do* refers to the acidity, from 0.6 in light sake to 2.8 for heavier sake. Serve warm or cold? This is really a matter of personal preference. If you prefer it warm, as we do, pour it into a heatproof pitcher and place in a pan of water over gentle heat, but be careful not to let it boil.

oven temperatures

Celsius*	Fahrenheit	Gas	Description
110°C	225°F	mark ¼	cool
130°C	250°F	mark ½	cool
140°C	275°F	mark 1	very low
150°C	300°F	mark 2	very low
170°C	325°F	mark 3	low
180°C	350°F	mark 4	moderate
190°C	375°F	mark 5	moderate-hot
200°C	400°F	mark 6	hot
220°C	425°F	mark 7	hot
230°C	450°F	mark 8	very hot

* For fan-assisted ovens, reduce temperatures by 10°C

volume

5ml	1 teaspoon
10ml	1 dessert spoon
15ml	1 tablespoon
30ml	1fl oz
50ml	2fl oz
75ml	3fl oz
100ml	3½fl oz
125ml	4fl oz
150ml	5fl oz (¼ pint)
200ml	7fl oz (⅓ pint)
250ml (¼ liter)	9fl oz
300ml	10fl oz (½ pint)
350ml	12fl oz
400ml	14fl oz
425ml	15fl oz (¾ pint)
450ml	16fl oz
500ml (½ liter)	18fl oz
600ml	1 pint (20fl oz)
700ml	1¼ pints
850ml	1½ pints
1 liter	1¾ pints
1.2 liters	2 pints
1.5 liters	2½ pints
1.8 liters	3 pints
2 liters	3½ pints

weight

10g	½ oz
20g	¾ oz
25g	1oz
50g	2oz
60g	2½ oz
75g	3oz
100g	3½ oz
110g	4oz (¼ lb)
150g	5oz
175g	6oz
200g	7oz
225g	8oz (½ lb)
250g (¼ kg)	9oz
275g	10oz
350g	12oz (¾ lb)
400g	14oz
450g	1lb
500g (½ kg)	18oz
600g	1¼ lb
700g	1½ lb
900g	2lb
1kg	2¼ lb
1.1kg	2½ lb
1.3kg	3lb
1.5kg	3lb 5oz
1.6kg	3½ lb
1.8kg	4lb
2kg	4½ lb
2.2kg	5lb

measurements

3mm	⅛ in
5mm	¼ in
1cm	½ in
2cm	¾ in
2.5cm	1in
3cm	1¼ in
4cm	1½ in
5cm	2in
6cm	2½ in
7.5cm	2¾ in
9cm	3½ in
10cm	4in
11.5cm	4½ in
12.5cm	5in
15cm	6in
17cm	6½ in
18cm	7in
20.5cm	8in
23cm	9in
24cm	9½ in
25.5cm	10in
30.5cm	11in

index

useful addresses

While not at all comprehensive, the following shops are good sources of Asian ingredients and equipment:

Australia
Japanese and Asian food is widely available in Australia from any of the supermarkets in Chinatown, Sydney and around the country.

Belgium
Sun Wah
Van Wesenbekestraat 16–17
2060 Antwerp

Holland
Toko Dun Yong
Stormsteeg 9
1012 BD Amsterdam

Yama Products
Rutherfordweg 2
3542 CG Utrecht

Ireland
Asia market
18 Drury Street
Dublin 2

Oriental Emporium
25 South Great Georges Street
Dublin 2

United Kingdom
Any of the supermarkets in Chinatown, London.

Wing Yip
395 Edgware Road
London NW2 6LN

Oldham Road, Ancoats
Manchester M4 5HU

Hanson Chinese Supermarket
2 Carrington Street
Nottingham NG1 7FF

Okinami Japanese Shop
12 York Place
Brighton BN1 4GU

Lims Chinese Supermarket
63 Cambridge Street
Kelvingrove
Glasgow G3 6QX
Scotland

USA
Japanese and Asian food is widely available in the United States from any of the supermarkets in Chinatown and around the country.

acknowledgments

Noodling can be done on your own. But it is much more fun to share. A project of this size involves many. So, a thank you to all wagamama staff, whose first response is always a smile. This has made the task hugely enjoyable as well as rewarding. Wigmore Street: thank you for all those early openings and green tea. In no particular order: Jason Pettit, for his work on the recipes; Ron Lento, who helped to clarify a lot about ingredients; Steve Mangleshot, who reminded us all that noodles are fun and that they make our lives richer; and Sarah Lim, Mark Tilson, Gary Muslow, and Pierre Galiere, who all talked noodles and managed to make sense of them when I was tied in knots.

To the wagamama team leaders, led by Ian Neill, who, along with Jay Travis, introduced a guiding hand whenever one was needed—my thanks. To Paul O'Farrell, whose undaunting enthusiasm and good judgement enabled so much creativity to shine. Many thanks also to Glyn House and Steve Hill, who took time to explain all the pieces in their relevant areas, causing me much confusion along the way! To Vikki O'Neill, who does, speaks, and thinks with clarity and speed. Some might even call it straight talking. And Lisa King, who dived in with enthusiasm at just the right moment.

To Kyle Cathie, who defines independence in book publishing with elegance.

The team who worked directly on the project were: Jenny Wheatley, whose editing style makes a strength out of understatement; Jacque Malouf, who cooked and cooked and cooked and still seemed ready for more; and Tabitha Hawkins, whose style and opinions were so perfectly in tune with everything and everyone else. Lucy Gowans contributed clarity and strength both to the project and to the pages. Ditte Isager brought so much alive in the photographs, but particularly those parts that are so difficult to define. My thanks to you all. And for seeing the value in so much talk.

The process of testing recipes is a long one and both Sharon Hearne and Jo McAuley dived into the world of noodles with gusto. My thanks to you both.

Suzanne Doyle keeps me on the straight and narrow more of the time than I think she realizes. The smooth running of this book from my end is largely down to her. Thank you.

My biggest thanks, as ever, are to Sue, Tom, and Ruby. Without you, none of it would be worthwhile.